Sweden

Up North, Down to Earth

Much of the focus of this book has been to highlight the cornerstones of Swedish society: equality, sustainability and transparency to mention a few. Giving a general overview of Sweden and Swedish society, the authors have homed in on the latest and most telling trends. This short book might just change the way you view Sweden.

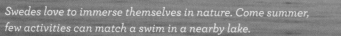

*Swedes love to immerse themselves in nature. Come summer,
few activities can match a swim in a nearby lake.*

Contents

Preface

Stepping Up to the Challenge

We Swedes speak up and put our collective foot down much more than people give us credit for. We are unafraid to push the boundaries that challenge both ourselves and others. We lobby hard for international agreements about the environment. We trust children to handle difficult subjects and emotions; so we don't protect them from topics like divorce or homosexuality. We have some of the strictest laws in the world against human trafficking, prostitution and drugs. We dare to be controversial.

We are used to seeing our country rank high on various global studies covering everything from broadband quality to responsible competitiveness. These studies confirm that Sweden is indeed a modern nation and part of the global community. Yet the journey from a poor agrarian society started less than a century ago, and in some ways part of the Swedish mentality holds on for dear life to its simple rural past. We are as fond of our traditions as we are of our modern lifestyle. Our relationship to the church is a point in case. Secular Swedes marry in church, and children are baptized there, more so for its traditional than religious meaning.

The change in Swedish society is ongoing. Swedes are some of the world's fastest at adapting to new trends and ideas. A curious and creative people with the means to change, it's no wonder we Swedes don't always recognize ourselves in the labels the world has assigned us: blond, quiet and homogenous, among others.

We are no more collectively blond than we are all internet pirates. Over the past fifty years or so, it's true that Sweden has seen a lot of change in its demographics, as almost a fifth of the population has roots in other countries. There is an ongoing migration of people in both directions.

The multicultural society brings a lot of good, but the short time-span in which Sweden has had to adjust has also presented some difficult challenges. The ugly face of cultural segregation is yet to be wiped out completely, but ethnic boundaries are increasingly crossed when it comes to anything from falling in love to working together or doing politics. At least the course is set for a Sweden without prejudice.

Snow and cold weather opens up for new ways to explore Stockholm.

DID YOU KNOW THAT

the lowest elevation in Sweden is in the bay of Lake Hammarsjön
at 7.9 ft/2.4 m below sea level, and the highest point is Kebnekaise
at 6,926 ft/2,111 m above sea level?

Sweden in Brief

Sweden is the third largest country in the European Union (EU) and comparable in size to Thailand and California. At 174,000 square miles/451,000 km², one can travel 978 miles/1,574 km north to south and 310 miles/499 km east to west as the crow flies. Over half of Sweden's area consists of forests, 11 percent of mountains and about 9 percent of rivers and lakes. All that open space and nature is a major underlying factor to our environmental awareness as well as our fondness of outdoor activities.

The open space also means quite a low population density; in fact only 53 people per square mile/21 per km² overall, but with a substantially higher density in the southern half of the country. Seen to population, roughly 9.3 million, Sweden is one of the smaller European nations but has been without population decrease since 1880. Sweden has one of the highest child birth rates in Europe and a fairly high immigration rate as well, with roughly 200 nationalities represented. In 2008, 14 percent of the population was born outside of Sweden.

The capital Stockholm is also the most populous city ahead of Gothenburg, Malmö and Uppsala. About 85 percent of the population lives in urban areas.

Swedish, which is the main language, is also an official language in Finland and the EU. Sweden, meanwhile, recognizes Sami, Finnish, Meänkieli (Torne Valley Finnish), Yiddish and Romani Chib as minority languages. Several other languages, such as Arabic and Polish, are also commonly heard, and we are often complemented on our English skills by native speakers.

Sweden is governed by parliamentary democracy and constitutional monarchy. The parliament (Riksdag) seats 349 members in one chamber. The separation of church and state goes well with the fact that Swedes are a mainly secularized people, a statement that may seem contradictory considering 70 percent of the population are still members of the Church of Sweden. While the Church of Sweden is Lutheran, it coexists with many other beliefs, practices and faiths. Upset Swedes more commonly turn to biblical rather than sexual references for cursing.

Although an EU member since 1995, we still pay with the krona (SEK) when we go shopping. We export a lot of machinery, electronics and telecommunication products and services, paper, pharmaceuticals, petroleum products, iron and steel. Our imports include electronics and telecommunication products, machinery, foodstuffs, crude oil, textiles and footwear.

Profile features of the Swedish society include a genuine strive for gender equality, children's rights, environmental protection, an accessible and accepting society, and democracy. Generally speaking, Swedes favor narrow economic gaps between social classes; yet that is a far cry from socialism as Sweden has a long history as a solid market economy.

Music festival season in Sweden is brief but intense, a time to let go of one's inhibitions.

The Turning Torso skyscraper has made a real impact on the Malmö skyline.

Nature

Our Cultural Heritage Is Nature

A performance of northern lights.

A large majority of us live in urban areas that are typically located in the southern half of the country, where we enjoy a vibrant cultural life, stay up to date with fashion and trends, and where the city pulse moves us forward at a lagom—just right—pace. If you ask a Swede to depict her or his environment, however, you will probably hear descriptions of scenic vistas, deep forests or a quiet island in the archipelago.

The reason is simply that we grow up appreciating the vast natural scenery that surrounds us, just around the corner from where we live, even if we live in a metropolitan area like Stockholm. There is something about Swedes and being out in the open, whether to exercise, get some fresh air or explore the countryside.

Surrounded by open and often astonishing nature, it is quite natural that Sweden should be at the forefront of sustainable solutions. Swedes are adamant that future generations should enjoy the same luxuries of wilderness and fresh air and water.

GEOGRAPHY

Home to some of the last and largest remaining wilderness areas in Europe, Sweden is characterized by dramatic changes in scenery even within a relatively small area. One could suggest the only constant is the foundation, as Sweden is situated in a geologically stable portion of the Eurasian land mass.

Much of our landscape is dominated by coniferous forests, often complemented by deciduous trees. These make for a beautiful autumn when the leaves burst into a final display of color and life before the barren winter. The southernmost landscape, Skåne, is home to Sweden's most fertile farmlands. A little further north it gives way to the forested highland region of Småland, surrounded by a varied pastoral countryside of fields and lakes.

Off the coast in the Baltic Sea lie Öland and Gotland, with some of the country's oldest and most fascinating historical sites. Orchids and other exotic flora make

the islands their home thanks to the lime-rich bedrock and favorable climate. The islands are popular vacation spots, particularly among Swedes. Other tourist magnets include the various archipelagos. People from the west and east coast argue the superior beauty of their respective archipelagos when in fact each coast is bestowed with its own unique charm.

Slightly further to the north we find Bergslagen, with ancient deposits of iron and other ores that once gave rise to Sweden's oldest industrial region. The area is not far

THE SAMI PEOPLE

The Sami make up one of the world's least numerous native peoples, with around 70,000 individuals living in Sápmi, in what is now parts of Sweden, Norway, Finland and Russia. About 20,000 Sami live in Sweden—with their own cultural heritage, language, flag and parliament.

Once nomadic hunters and gatherers who followed the movements of wild reindeer, the Sami increasingly began to drive domesticated reindeer between grazing lands in the 17th century. Besides reindeer herding and meat production, arts and handicrafts is another traditional trade that has survived into modern days. Most Sami, however, have jobs with no connection to the traditional way of life.

Although Sápmi remains the cultural heartland, the Sami people have spread out over the Nordic region and there are now as many Sami living in Stockholm as there are in the north of Sweden. Established in 1993, the Sami Parliament in Sweden is both a publicly elected body and a state authority, tasked with promoting a living Sami culture. It is not a body for self-government and the Sami have no political representation in the Swedish Parliament.

Ancient Sami mythology focuses on the natural elements like the sun (Biejvve), mother of the Sami, and the wind god (Bieggaålmaj), who made it possible to catch the reindeer. In their shamanistic beliefs, nature has a soul. The Sami still call themselves "The people of the sun and the wind."

Sami families outside Jokkmokk divide their reindeer ahead of the move to winter pasture.

Sarek National Park, an area of pure wilderness, stands out from most other parks by not having any facilities for tourists at all? So if you feel like really roughing it in the wild, you know where to go.

the Celsius temperature scale is named after Swedish astronomer Anders Celsius (1701–1744)? Water freezes at 0°C and boils at 100°C.

Here we are

The Arctic Circle

Kiruna

Umeå

FINLAND

NORWAY

SWEDEN

Gävle

Uppsala

Västerås

Örebro

Stockholm

Norrköping

Linköping

Borås
Göteborg
(Gothenburg)

Jönköping

Visby

Växjö

Helsingborg

Lund
Malmö

DENMARK

from Stockholm, a city of striking beauty spread across fourteen islands in Lake Mälaren. In 2007, the city controversially branded itself as the Capital of Scandinavia, upon which a blogger from Gothenburg responded, "Great, then we'll take over as capital of Sweden!"

To the northwest, the Scandinavian mountain range rises north and south like a fossil beast separating Norway from Sweden, its modest peaks rising 3,000–7,000 feet/1,000–2,000 meters above sea level, a sneak preview of what's up ahead in the true north.

Following the mountain range, one eventually reaches Lapland (Sápmi), home of one of Europe's few remaining native people, the Sami. It's an area of stunning grandeur, a vast landscape of true wilderness, at once serene, dramatic and untamed. The rapidly changing weather and steep topography make visiting the mountain areas a challenge. It's unwise to venture off the beaten track in places like the Sarek National Park without genuine back-country hiking experience. Those who do will have an experience far beyond the ordinary.

Sweden's largest rivers originate in the mountains, and on their way to the Baltic Sea, they pass a mixture of polar plains, meadows, coniferous and birch forests, and marshes; in short, they pass through the poetic grandeur of the Arctic landscape until they reach the coastline dappled by islands and islets.

	JANUARY	JULY	DECEMBER 21	JUNE 21
			W SOLSTICE	S SOLSTICE
MALMÖ	31.6°F/-0.2°C	62.2°F/+16.8°C	7 hrs daylight	17 hours
STOCK-HOLM	27.0°F/-2.8°C	63.0°F/+17.2°C	6 hrs daylight	18 hours
KIRUNA	3.2°F/-16.0°C	55.0°F/+12.8°C	0 hrs daylight	24 hours

Average temperatures

WEATHER AND CLIMATE

Swedes ought to give thanks to the Gulf Stream every day; after all, the misconception that polar bears roam the Swedish landscape could actually be true were it not for this warm Atlantic current that delivers us from freezing. Sweden is also sheltered from cooler and moister Atlantic winds by the mountains to our west.

Still, we do have four distinct seasons, and the winters can be very cold, especially if you venture as far as the northernmost third, or for that matter follow a brazen Swede from the warmth of a sauna and plunge into a frozen lake.

Much more extreme than the fabled Swedish weather is what happens to the light during the shifting seasons. Throughout Sweden the length of daylight increases as spring approaches, and the area most affected is the north (heavy curtains or eye shades come in handy, especially in June and July). Above the Arctic Circle the sun does not set for a month or two around summer solstice. Further south the few hours of darkness provided are more like an afterglow. The opposite is true for the winter months.

To pierce the darkness up north, besides using fairly huge amounts of electric light, the snow helps with reflection and occasionally the *aurora borealis* will play across the sky. This visual symphony of northern lights is one of the most beautiful and spectacular sights around, formed when electrically charged particles are thrust into the earth's magnetic field at great speed, propelled by solar winds.

NATIONAL PARKS

To protect its vast natural scenery and cultural heritage from exploitation, Sweden was the first European country to set up a nature conservation act and establish national parks: nine of them opened in 1909. A century later the number had grown to 29.

The Laponia wilderness area beckons hikers to get lost in their thoughts.

The parks constitute large areas representative of Swedish landscape types such as astonishing mountainous regions, which make up roughly 90 percent of the total park area. Others include wetlands, forests, lakes, streams, coastal regions, and—most recently—our first marine national park, Kosterhavet. Laponia is a conglomeration of four national parks in western Lapland, included in UNESCO's World Heritage List.

Another form of protection is achieved through nature reserves, many of which are set up in order to preserve natural habitats and the species that live there, or in order to promote outdoor life, or why not both? We currently have about 3,200 reserves that lure us out into nature.

The government and local municipalities go to great extents to protect the environment, and so do the people who live here. Voluntary efforts, sometimes with financial support from the government, are an important complement to official conservation. Over the past hundred years, a lot has been done, but much of the work also remains. Luckily, the majority of Swedes are both aware of the situation and up for the challenge.

ANIMALS AND VEGETATION

As a result of specific long-term efforts to protect endangered and rare animals, our grazers, birds and animals of prey have been given a second chance after decades of uninhibited hunting. Any plant or animal that is in danger of extinction may be given protected status by the Swedish Environmental Protection Agency in addition to the shelter afforded through national parks and nature reserves.

The moose is not only a noble animal that lives throughout most forested parts of Sweden, but also a common souvenir motif, a traffic hazard, popular game, and food for our most common animals of prey: the brown bear, wolverine, wolf and lynx. Although the other animals in what could be called Sweden's Big Five are all predators, it is perhaps the moose that is the most aggressive towards (or least afraid of) people. When it comes to wildlife management of our predators, the wolf remains the most controversial—loved or feared. In 2010 the first licensed wolf hunt in 45 years took place, not without a fierce debate.

Wintertime, bird life in Sweden is dominated by a few species, but with spring and summer a large number of migratory birds from more southerly climates join these permanent residents. With its long coastline and many lakes, Sweden also has a rich variety of waterborne life, from fish species to seals.

Sweden's flora is also quite varied, from dandelions to exotic orchids, particularly in the mountains and on the Baltic islands of Gotland and Öland. Perhaps better known than the plants is 18th-century physician and botanist Carl Linnaeus, who is considered one of the most important forerunners of Darwin and who created the first classification system for plants, *Systema Naturae*.

ACCESSING NATURE

With so much grandeur and open space to enjoy, Swedes would be foolish not to take advantage of it. And we do, come rain, snow, wind or sun, defending our reasoning with the saying, "There is no bad weather, only poor clothing." After all, what better way of enjoying nature than to take active advantage of it? And depending on taste, that could mean anything from picking chanterelles to ascending a frozen waterfall.

The wolf has been an integral part of the Scandinavian ecosystem since after the last Ice Age.

Sailboats moor at natural harbors in the archipelago by Väderöarna on the west coast.

the limestone rocks on the island of
Gotland are locally called raukar?
Many of them are in fact very old
coral reefs.

DID YOU KNOW THAT

Uppsala University researchers have for the past six years been working on a unique wave-power technology that is now ready to go into production? The Uppsala technology turns the power of waves into electrical energy without emissions or harmful waste, and all you can see on the surface of the sea is a number of giant yellow buoys.

It's not just that we live in a sparsely populated region of natural beauty. Since 1892 we have had a national organization for promoting outdoor activities; we are quite health conscious; and we are probably even more environmentally conscious. With more people taking part in nature, there is also an opportunity to get more people to care about preserving it for future generations. In Sweden, making the outdoors more accessible goes hand in hand with informing about its vulnerability.

Furthermore, *allemansrätten*, the unique Swedish right of public access which is a part of our cultural heritage and has its origins in the Middle Ages, allows people to go pretty much anywhere in nature without coming across entrance fees or fences, and to pick most wild foods off the ground along the way. With this right comes a huge responsibility—to take care of nature and wildlife and to show consideration for landowners and others. Basically, we can be out and about as long as we don't disturb or destroy.

Sweden is a haven for winter sports. Frozen lakes, public skating rinks and forests are quickly invaded by skaters and cross-country skiers. Cabins in the mountains are booked by downhill enthusiasts. And more and more are discovering the rush of adrenaline through kite wing

skating, ice yachting or ice climbing. Winter sports are technically not limited to the wintertime: Midsummer downhill skiing is popular north of the Arctic Circle. A pretty unique experience considering the sun never sets over the slopes during this time of year.

Of course most people don't go skiing in the summertime. People head into the woods to pick berries or mushrooms, hike into the mountains for a backpacking trek, go sailing or kayaking in the archipelago or set off white-river rafting on one of Sweden's many first-class rivers. Whether on the look for peace and tranquility or a fix of adrenaline, these practitioners all share a love for the outdoors.

Even while big-city tourism is the fastest-growing segment, Sweden is, as you might have guessed by now, a major center for ecotourism, and our natural splendor is the number one attraction among foreign visitors from more densely populated parts of the world.

SUSTAINABLE CITY PLANNING

Sweden has a reputation of being an environmental leader. Sustainability certainly lies close to our hearts, but we are also one of the world's largest per capita consumers of electricity. In our defense, we are informed consumers and dedicated to reduce our environmental footprint. One of the few industrialized countries to reduce carbon emissions over the last decades, Sweden will improve these levels further and has committed to become a fossil-fuel free society by 2020.

Sustainable city planning has also helped justify the global attention that falls on Sweden's environmental work. Hammarby Sjöstad has incorporated sustainability into the planning of electricity, water, sewage and refuse. This Stockholm neighborhood is also furnished with open areas and ecological trade spots.

A new eco-friendly area is underway for the north-

east of Stockholm. People working and living in Norra Djurgårdsstaden will be connected to the world's first "smart" power lines that ensure reliance on clean power by saving energy, using locally produced clean energy and avoiding peak hours (programming household machines like dishwashers to run during off-peak hours).

This kind of comprehensive approach to an ecologically sound environment can be found throughout Sweden. Växjö, a small city in the south, is an internationally recognized forerunner in the environmental field. It was a massive restoration of Lake Växjö in the 1970s that got the town thinking. The lake is now used for recreation such as swimming, fishing and lakeside walks.

Växjö has pledged to go much further than the EU directives when it comes to reducing the amount of carbon dioxide released into the atmosphere—at least 70 percent by 2025. Sarah Nilsson, an environmental planner at the Växjö municipality, notices a continued interest in their approach: "We receive visits from about five groups per week, three of which are international. So the interest and the pressure on our organization is high. Sometimes we try to catch our breath but most of the time it's great fun."

Swedes learn recycling from an early age.

Erosion has worked the design of these limestone rocks on Gotland.

VÄXJÖ—THE GREENEST CITY IN EUROPE

There are several fueling stations with alternative fuels like ethanol (E85) and bio fuels and free parking for "green" vehicles.

Energy efficiency can be accomplished with fairly simple measures, as illustrated by the project Biskopshagen: apartments and a nursery school fitted with proper insulation, recycling of heat from extraction air, and individual metering of heat, water and electricity.

The energy advisor's office, EnergiCentrum-Ett, provides free information and advice on different energy-saving solutions.

Vehicle positioning systems for commercial trucks and taxis optimizes transport and reduces the movement of empty vehicles.

Bicycle paths and lanes are expanded to facilitate cycling and increase bike traffic.

MALMÖ 200   STOCKHOLM 445

The Johansson family, whom you will get to know better in the next chapter, have received financial support for installing solar panels on their Växjö house and have replaced their oil-heating system with distance heating. They separate recyclables and have compost in their yard. Their car is only used for weekend trips as they bike and walk to work and school. The Johanssons live a regular Växjö life.

VÄXJÖ

Passive houses—apartments such as those found in the Portvakten Söder area—are constructed with a wood frame with no traditional heating system, only insulation and heating from people and appliances. The roofs are fitted with solar panels, elevators are energy-efficient, and all lights use low-energy bulbs connected to timers.

Public transport is encouraged and city buses run on biogas.

Växjö has a number of timber construction projects of which Välle Broar is the most cohesive, with energy-efficient and well-insulated apartments with a framework entirely of timber. Choosing timber frames over concrete greatly reduces the net emissions of CO_2.

CHP (combined heat and power) plants such as Sandvik rely almost exclusively on biomass. The ashes that follow the smoke are caught in a filter and used as fertilizer. Waste heat is captured and distributed through a network of buried, insulated pipes to heat buildings. The plant also produces cooling from heat via a new technique called absorption cooling.

Solar panels are fitted on public and private buildings. Those on the main public swimming pool are even recycled from a demolished building while those fitted on a school building are also used in the curriculum: in mathematics for cost analysis, in physics as a hands-on example of renewable energy sources, and in English for when international visitors stop by for a look at the eco-town Växjö.

- Between 1993 and 2008 Växjö has reduced its CO_2 emissions by 35 percent.
- 56 percent of energy comes from renewable sources (2008).
- 46 percent of families in Växjö do not own a private car (2008).

The Stockholm Pride festival has become a symbol of Swedish tolerance.

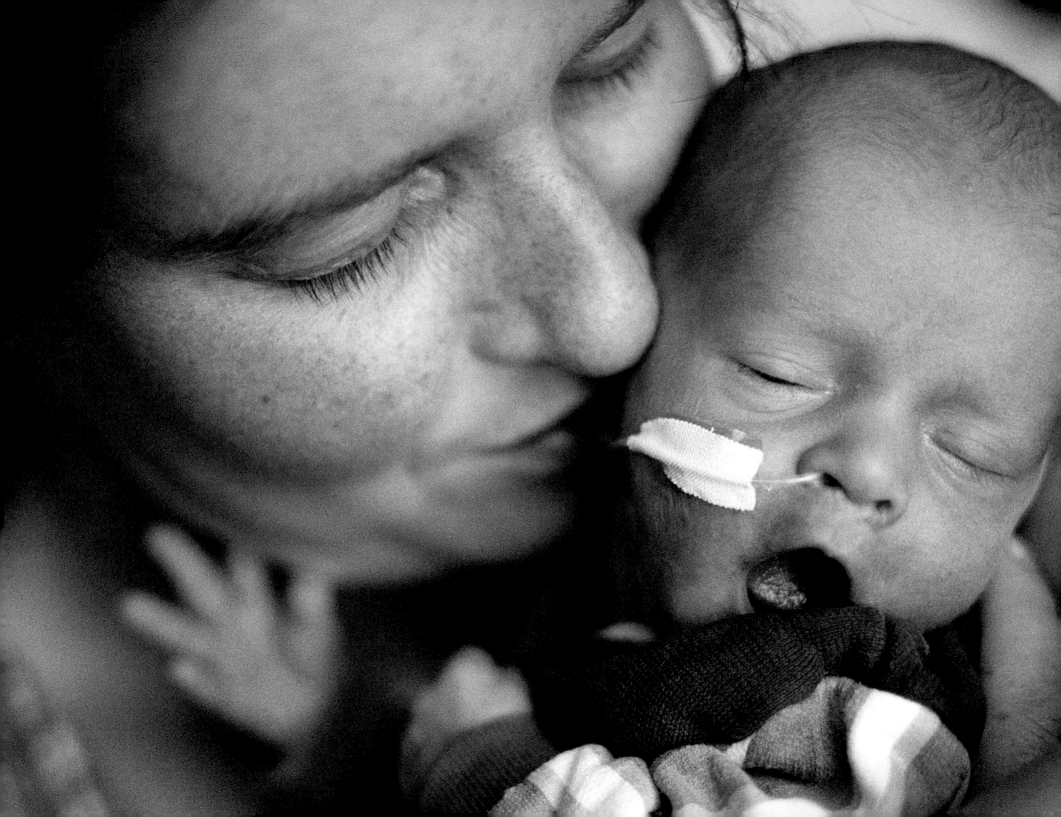

Society

Grounded on Democracy, Striving for Equality and Tolerance

Modern Sweden is solidly founded on democracy. Democratic principles shape not only the way the country is governed, but all levels of society—from preschool to the workplace. We also fly the flag for equality and transparency. Everyone has the same rights and a chance to have their say, and we are all free to scrutinize how our politicians and public agencies exercise their power.

Sweden's economic and social system, often referred to as the "Swedish Model," has lifted the country to one of the highest standards of living in the world. By combining a market economy with a strong public sector the country ensures equality and financial security for each and every individual. Even though the economic situation for the public sector has become tougher over the last decades and its general structure is being debated, the Swedish safety net is still there—although somewhat weakened. Tax-financed education and health care contribute to making Sweden a role model for many other countries.

SWEDES

To illustrate the Swedish Model, we want to introduce you to the average Swedish family, the Johanssons: Anna Maria, 42, Lars Erik, 39, Simon, 15, and Emma, 12. This family, their names and their life is a fictional construction, based on statistical averages for Sweden as reported by Statistics Sweden as well as other facts. For example, 272,594 Swedes are named Johansson, which makes this the most common surname.

The Johanssons live in the small city of Växjö (280 miles, or 450 kilometers, south-west of Stockholm) in a house with a tax-assessed value of SEK 963,000, which equals around 75 percent of the market value. They have

chosen to live in Växjö mainly because of the city's focus on sustainability and its proximity to nature. More than four-fifths of Swedes live in cities, and two-thirds live in houses, one-third in apartments. The Johanssons also have a summer house in the country, along with half of the 35 to 44-year-olds. Their silver-colored Volvo takes them to and from the summer house.

With their two children, the Johanssons have slightly

> ### DID YOU KNOW THAT
> **the average Swedish family eats 2.6 lbs/1.2 kg of sweets per week? On the other hand, more than 60 percent of Swedes claim to be physically active more than 30 minutes a day.**

more than the 2008 average of 1.9 children per woman. The fact that Lars has been married to Anna for fourteen years also sets him apart from the unmarried majority of 39-year-old men in Sweden. Many unmarried Swedes are in a *sambo* relationship, that is, live together with a partner without being married. And did you know that almost half of the Swedish households are single households? The reason why Anna is older than Lars in our average couple is that women have a higher life expectancy. In real life, it is actually more common that the man is one or two years older than the woman.

Anna works in the care sector, earning SEK 20,900 per month. Lars makes SEK 26,400 per month in the production industry. After taxes, they have a monthly income

of SEK 35,600 together. Add to this a tax-exempt child allowance from the state of SEK 1,050 per month and child. Emma and Simon in turn get a monthly allowance from their parents of SEK 220 and 600, respectively. (Simon gets more simply because he is older, not because he is a boy.)

When Simon and Emma were babies, in 1991 and 1994, both Anna and Lars used their right to parental leave. Today parents are entitled to as much as 480 paid days at home with each of their children; back then, the period was slightly shorter. The signal is clear: it is important for both parents to be able to combine a career with having children. By implementing generous rules and benefits, Swedish society has made this possible. A male employee announcing that he wants to go on paternity leave hardly raises any eyebrows anymore. In 2008, men used around 20 percent of the total parental leave—more than twice as much as when Simon was born.

The individual is at the center of elderly care.

Lucky baby! Your parents can stay home with you for 480 days.

23

EDUCATION AND RESEARCH

Equal rights to tuition-free education from the age of six is one of the pillars of the Swedish welfare state. And from the very first day at school we are encouraged to think for ourselves and develop our critical thinking.

When Simon and Emma started preschool at the age of one and a half, state subsidies ensured that Anna and Lars only had to pay a limited cost for it. In 2009's figures, this means that preschool never costs parents more than 3 percent of their income (or at most SEK 1,260) per month, a rule that applies to public as well as private preschools. Thus affordable for all, the idea is that preschools stimulate children's development and learning, while enabling parents to work or study.

At the age of six, most children start school, but only a non-compulsory preschool class. As seven-year-olds, Simon and Emma started their nine years of free compulsory schooling. Apart from regular primary and secondary schools, compulsory schooling also includes Sami school—with education in both Swedish and Sami for children with Sami parents; special school for children with disabilities; and programs for pupils with intellectual disabilities. There are also non-municipal—but still tax-financed—independent schools in many areas. They offer a similar basic education, but with a more specific focus, such as language, religion or a certain pedagogy.

From the age of six, Simon and Emma went straight from school to the after-school day care, a service offered to children up to twelve that takes a load off full-time-working parents' shoulders. The fee for this type of day care is limited to a maximum of 2 percent of the parents' income.

Until recently, students were only given grades from the eighth grade, but some schools have now begun to offer written evaluations at a younger age. Simon is in the ninth grade. He will use his final grades to apply for the Social Science Program at the non-compulsory but equally free-of-charge high school. Around 98 percent of students who finish compulsory school go on to high school. For those who attend high school, the child allowance is from the age of sixteen transformed into a monthly study allowance.

Simon is not yet clear about what he wants to do after high school. Perhaps he will take a gap year before doing like hundreds of thousands of his peers and give university studies a go. Why wouldn't he? Even higher education is fully tax-financed for him. Moreover, if he decides to study at university he will also be eligible for financial student aid, which is part grant, part loan.

Sweden has a proud history of academic excellence that dates back to the founding of the University of Uppsala in 1477. Today, Swedish universities are characterized by a laid-back atmosphere, where relations

SNILLEBLIXTARNA—LEARNING THROUGH INNOVATION

Snilleblixtarna ("Flashes of Genius") is a Swedish teaching model that aims to put the fun back into science and technology. It encourages school children to be creative and develop their problem-solving skills, thus giving the children higher self-esteem. Every year a huge number of their amazing innovations are exhibited at a national fair. How about a pair of self-sanding shoes, for example, for those slippery Swedish winter days?

Self-Sanding Shoes
For slippery days

Andreas, Felix & Salim 11 years old

SEX	POPULATION	LEVEL OF EDUCATION *(percentages)*			
		Compulsory education (age 7–16)	High school	Higher education: shorter than 3 years	Higher education: 3 years or longer
WOMEN	2,389,451	13	45	15	26
MEN	2,457,670	17	48	14	19
ALL	4,847,121	15	46	14	22

Level of education among people in Sweden aged 25–64 (2008)

between students and teachers are open and informal. But don't get the wrong idea—Sweden is renowned for its high education standards. Teachers simply encourage students to use their own initiative rather than tell them exactly what to do. Most likely, the prestigious Nobel Prize has played a part in convincing us that innovation is the way forward.

HEALTH CARE AND SOCIAL SECURITY

The Swedish health care system is closely linked to social insurance, which means that everyone who lives or works in Sweden has access to heavily subsidized health care.

If Anna or Lars falls ill, it is of course a nuisance but not a financial disaster for the family. Sick-leave pay from your employer normally amounts to 80 percent of your salary, apart from the first day, when you don't get paid at all. If they are ill for more than fourteen days, they will get a slightly lower sickness benefit from the Swedish Social Insurance Agency. For longer-term illnesses, the entitlement to sickness benefit will be assessed at regular intervals.

When Anna and Lars go to see a doctor, they only pay a fee of between SEK 100 and 200 depending on the county, or a maximum of SEK 300 for a specialist visit. The fee for staying in a hospital is SEK 80 per day. High-cost ceilings also limit the yearly cost for both medical consultations (SEK 900) and prescription medication (SEK 1,800).

Most health care is provided in health centers, where doctors, nurses and other staff work together. The Johanssons have all registered with a health center in the vicinity of their home in Växjö. Responsibility for providing health care is decentralized to the counties and, in some cases, municipalities. A growing number of private health care providers in Sweden are starting to compete with the public care facilities. The clever thing is that the social insurance covers them as well, so the cost to the patient is the same.

Dental care is not quite as subsidized as other health care, and the dentists decide on their own treatment prices. But social insurance still pays for Simon's and Emma's check-ups or treatments—until the year they turn twenty. From then on, they will receive a dental care allowance and will be protected by a high-cost ceiling.

Should Anna or Lars lose their job, they will receive unemployment pay linked to their previous salary because they are members of an unemployment insurance program. Without insurance, they would still be entitled to an activity grant from the Social Insurance Agency, but that would mean less money.

An income support benefit provides for those who are not entitled to unemployment pay/activity grant nor sick pay/sickness benefit. This benefit is intended to be a short-term solution to help people get back on their feet. Low-income families are also able to apply for housing allowance.

With quite a few years to go, Lars and Anna have already started talking about the financial implications of retirement. They are happy to know that Sweden invests more of its gross domestic product in its elderly citizens than any other country in the world. All Swedish residents are entitled to a state-financed guaranteed minimum pension from the age of 65, which is the standard retirement age in Sweden. Since Lars and Anna are both employed, they will automatically receive an income pension instead, as well as an employment-based pension that their employer contributes to throughout their working life. But to make sure that they can sustain their relatively high living standard, they complement these pensions with private savings.

Life expectancy in Sweden is about 83 years for women and 79 for men. Anna's parents are pushing 75, and the Johanssons have started looking into elderly care for them. Swedes are so used to their independent lives that arranging elderly care for your parents is all about finding the best solution to allow your parents to keep leading active lives. Anna's parents will probably be able to stay in their own home, where they can get access to public support, including home meal delivery, help with cleaning and shopping, transportation service, as well as social and health care when needed. Should their health deteriorate with age, there is also special housing with around-the-clock care. Most of the elderly care is provided by municipalities, some by private operators.

THE LABOR MARKET

The Swedish work climate is generally open and informal. We call the boss by her or his first name, encour-

● COUNTY DEVELOPMENT: 112 (3)
○ DENTAL CARE: 102 (3)
◔ POLITICAL ORGANIZATION: 19 (0.5)
◑ EDUCATION*: 13 (0.5)
● OTHER: 91 (2.5)

*Continuing education for employees of the county of Kronoberg.

HEALTH CARE: 3,320 (90.5)

Public spending, in MSEK and %, in the county of Kronoberg (2008)

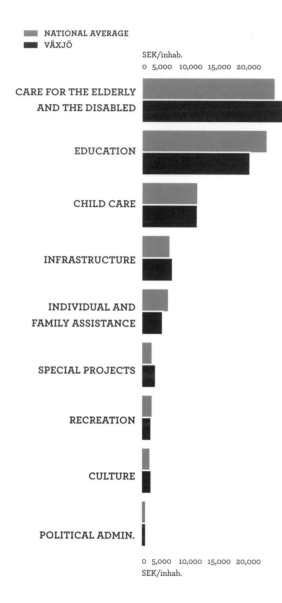

SEK/inhab.

0   5,000   10,000   15,000   20,000

CARE FOR THE ELDERLY
AND THE DISABLED

EDUCATION

CHILD CARE

INFRASTRUCTURE

INDIVIDUAL AND
FAMILY ASSISTANCE

SPECIAL PROJECTS

RECREATION

CULTURE

POLITICAL ADMIN.

0   5,000   10,000   15,000   20,000
SEK/inhab.

Public expenditure in SEK per inhabitant in the municipality of Växjö (2007)

age teamwork, have flexible work hours, dress casually and strive for gender equality. A long tradition of active labor market policies and powerful unions has resulted in a strong protection of workers' rights and a great number of benefits for Swedish employees.

With the history of Swedish trade and labor unions reaching as far back as the late 1800s, almost 80 percent of Swedish workers are union members, including private-sector worker Lars and public-sector employee Anna. One of the unions' main roles is to drive and support collective bargaining. This is a system in which unions negotiate with employers to establish a set of rights—ranging from wage and vacation agreements to the right to go on strike—that apply to all employees at a workplace.

As a health-care employee of the county council of Kronoberg, Anna enjoys as many as 31 days of paid vacation a year since she turned 40. Lars, who works in the production industry, has the legal minimum of 25 days' vacation. On the other hand, Lars always has the twelve national holidays off, whereas Anna sometimes has to work due to the irregular work schedules in the care sector.

At least a couple of times a year, Anna and Lars are offered to go on a course. This is part of a well-developed system of continuing education that is aimed at ensuring that all employees get a chance to develop, both as professionals and as individuals. Swedish employees have collective agreements to thank for many of their employment benefits.

The safety of the working environment is the shared responsibility of employers, employees and equipment suppliers, and the regulations can be found in the Work Environment Act. The act also contains measures to restrict hazards, prevent accidents and in other ways protect the physical and mental health of employees.

Apart from being safe, Swedish workplaces are also known for their fairness, honesty and transparency.

Corporate social responsibility (CSR) is central to Swedish businesses, which a widespread concern for the environment, human rights and anticorruption bears witness to. Call it pretentious if you like, but Swedes believe that a responsible approach to business can change society and the environment for the better.

By now, you may have figured out that although the Johanssons' monthly income may be fairly low in comparison with some of the other industrialized countries, they have managed to achieve a very high living standard thanks to all the tax-financed public services they have access to.

EQUALITY

According to the Global Gender Gap Report issued annually by the World Economic Forum, Sweden is one

WELCOME, GLOBAL WORKERS!

Since December 2008, Sweden has more relaxed labor migration laws for non-Nordic, non-EU/EEA and non-Swiss residents. The new approach to work permit legislation is unique. From abroad, someone can find a job in Sweden, receive an offer of employment, and get a Swedish work permit. After only four years, permanent residency can be granted. These new rules are aimed at helping Sweden attract the best talent available in the fast-changing global labor market.

TOP BUSINESS SECTORS

Sweden's largest private sectors include cleantech, information and communication technologies (ICT), life sciences, the automotive industry and material sciences. Naturally, forestry and such public sectors as health care also continue to employ a large number of people.

A Johansson family at the beach.

The five most common occupations among women (2007)

OCCUPATION	NUMBER OF		SHARE (%)		
	WOMEN	MEN	WOMEN	MEN	
Assistant nurses and hospital ward assistants	148,600	11,700	93	7	
Home-based personal care and related workers	135,000	25,500	84	16	
Childcare workers	85,300	10,900	89	11	
Preschool teaching professionals	74,900	6,200	92	8	
Other office clerks	73,500	19,600	79	21	

The five most common occupations among men (2007)

OCCUPATION	NUMBER OF		SHARE (%)		
	WOMEN	MEN	MEN	WOMEN	
Technical and commercial sales representatives	60,000	23,000	72	28	
Heavy truck and lorry drivers	54,100	1,800	97	3	
Computer systems designers, analysts and programmers	51,800	14,100	79	21	
Stock clerks and storekeepers	47,200	11,000	81	19	
Machine-tool operators	43,900	5,600	89	11	

The office, Swedish style: we speak our mind and work as a team.

of the world leaders in equality between the sexes. Both women and men are entitled to parental leave, women's salaries amount to about 93 percent of men's and many spouses share responsibilities in the home. In addition, around 80 percent of all women aged 20–64 are working (figures from 2007), a remarkably high figure in international comparison.

It seems rather uncontroversial to claim that family-friendly policies, such as the accessible and affordable childcare that has allowed families like the Johanssons more flexibility in their lives, have contributed to Sweden's relatively high fertility rate of 1.9 children per woman (compared with the European average of 1.5 children). Women like Anna Johansson don't have to choose between pursuing a career and having children; the public sector makes sure they can have both.

So, all good in the paradise of equality, then? No, not quite. Although women may be getting more and more power among private businesses, they are still in the minority on the board and management levels, and companies are criticized for not doing enough to improve the balance between the sexes. On the other hand, the majority of managers in municipalities, county councils and central government are women, as well as almost 50 percent of members of the Swedish government and parliament.

Of course, equality covers more than gender gaps; it's about offering everyone the same chances regardless of sex, ethnic origin, religion or other belief, disability, sexual orientation or age. Sweden has a long history of promoting equal rights for all through legislation and by openly taking a stand against all kinds of discrimination. This is why many Swedes react very strongly against the appearance of xenophobic parties on the political scene and why racist demonstrations are always met with strong opposition.

A global obstacle to equality is human trafficking. Sweden has taken action against this dreadful trade by implementing strict legislation. First we criminalized those who purchase sex; then we specifically banned human trafficking for sexual purposes, a law that was subsequently extended to include other forms of exploitation as well. And in 2008, the government decided to distribute more public funding to intensify the efforts to combat prostitution and human trafficking for sexual purposes. These Swedish actions and policies are inspiring many other countries to get tougher.

In 2009, Sweden took another important step toward a more equal society: same-sex marriage was

MILESTONES OF SWEDISH GENDER EQUALITY

1845: Equal inheritance rights for women and men.

1921: Women get the right to vote and run for office.

1938: Contraception is legalized.

1965: Sweden passes a law against rape in marriage.

1974: Parental insurance is introduced, granting both parents the right to parental leave.

1975: A new abortion law permits free abortions through the 18th week.

1980: Female (i.e. gender-neutral) succession to the throne comes into effect.

1980: The Office of the Equal Opportunities Ombudsman is introduced (became part of the Equality Ombudsman in 2009).

1998: The Act on Violence against Women is introduced.

1999: A new law forbids the purchase of sexual services.

2002: Human trafficking for sexual purposes is criminalized.

legalized—with support from the Church of Sweden. Registered partnership for homosexuals was introduced already in 1995, but the gender-neutral view on marriage means that gay and lesbian couples who get married now have the same legal status as people in heterosexual marriages.

We also have laws aimed at protecting children's rights, both in society and in the home. In 1979, many other countries considered Sweden radical—perhaps even mad—when it became the first country in the world to ban parents from spanking their children.

DEMOCRACY

Perhaps the whole point of democracy and freedom is to be able to discover things for oneself—and be allowed to fail. We Swedes may be somewhat overzealous when it comes to rules, maybe because we see most of them as a necessity to ensure an equal and just society. Turns out we are just as zealous when it comes to defending our freedoms.

Two laws recently introduced brought the Swedish public to the edge of their seats: the FRA law, which authorized the government to monitor all computer and telephone communications between Sweden and the outside world, and the IPRED law, which is an attempt to curb internet piracy. The laws were controversial but the public reactions revealed a lot about our adamant defense of our freedoms.

In Sweden we enjoy a free press, the right to participate in demonstrations, freedom of speech and the right to scrutinize those in power. In 1766, when Sweden enacted the world's first freedom of press act, it was a radical move. The Swedish laws ensuring freedom of information and especially public transparency are still turning a few international heads.

Transparency reduces the risk of abuse of power.

Sweden's top rankings over the years as one of the least corrupt nations indicates that this logic stands. Sweden takes transparency to new heights: laws give the general public and media access to official records, including everything down to emails sent within a government agency, and requires the information to be easy to understand and free of charge. Of course, some things such as national security can be classified, but on the whole, if it is official it is available to anyone who asks. The principle of public access also means that government employees are free to inform the media on their own initiative.

To further ensure public transparency the Swedish government has since 1809 used the ombudsman system—public agencies that represent the interests of individuals or groups. Among other things, an ombudsman investigates constituent complaints. Specifically, the Parliamentary Ombudsman handles complaints against a public authority or civil servant. The Equality Ombudsman promotes equal rights and fights all forms of discrimination due to ethnical background, gender, sexual preference, or disability. People who feel they have been misled by an advertising campaign have an ombudsman to turn to, and there are also separate ombudsman offices for children and for the press.

Of course most of these rights also require responsibility from those who enjoy it. Freedom of speech can be seen as offensive or have negative consequences for an individual or society. With a global information flow through the internet, we Swedes also have to take into consideration the reactions from other countries, and be prepared to explain and justify our rights to people with different values. These laws are in place to ensure human rights and freedoms for all. Public power should always be exercised with respect for the equality of all and for the freedom of the individual.

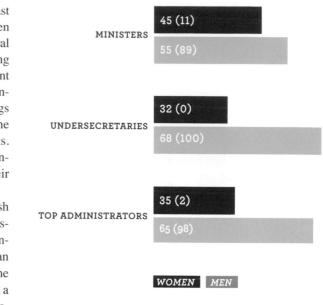

Gender distribution of top officials in government offices in March 2008 (percentages for 1973 in brackets)

THE SOCIALIST GHOST

There is an exaggerated rumor about Sweden being a socialist country, alluding to the threatening communist East of the Cold War. While it is true that the Social Democrats ruled Sweden for most of the 20th century, Sweden has been a market economy for a long time, with a vast majority of Swedish businesses being privately owned. Public–private cooperation is increasingly common and we no longer have any inheritance tax or wealth tax. Moreover, the Swedish tax on real estate is low compared with other countries. We do, on the other hand, still pay enough taxes to get access to a wide range of free and subsidized public services—education, health care, infrastructure and so on. Is this why the 2009 Eurobarometer survey showed that 96 percent of Swedes are satisfied with the life they lead?

Reaction against the FRA legislation outside the parliament building.

GOVERNMENT

All power proceeds from the people. This is the foundation of the parliamentary democracy in Sweden, even though the country is formally ruled by a government. The 349 members of the Swedish parliament (Riksdag) represent the people and the government answers to the parliament. The parliament has the legislative power and the government the executive power. In other words, the parliament makes the decisions and the government implements them, but also submits proposals for new laws or amendments to laws to the parliament.

Every four years, we have free, universal and equal elections where we vote for our preferred representatives to the national, regional and local governments. In international comparisons election turnout is normally high, even though it has fallen to about 80 percent in recent decades. Citizens of an EU country, Norway or Iceland have the right to vote in elections to the municipality and county where they are registered. This also applies to other foreign citizens aged at least 18 who have been registered in Sweden for at least three years. To vote in a parliamentary election, you must be a Swedish citizen aged at least 18 registered or previously registered in Sweden. Most Swedish citizens living abroad are also eligible to vote.

After the parliamentary elections, the speaker of the parliament suggests a new prime minister based on who has the strongest political support in the new parliament. The parliament then formally appoints the suggested prime minister, who in turn appoints the ministers for the new government.

The Social Democrats governed Sweden for most of the 20th century, but over the last few decades power has shifted back and forth between them and the four main opposing parties—the Moderates, Liberals, Center and Christian Democrats.

Swedish governance as a whole is built on decentralization. On a local and regional level, the municipalities and the county councils are autonomous political bodies with clearly defined areas of responsibility. The local councils deal with, for example, city planning and schools, while the county councils are in charge of areas such as health care and infrastructure.

Since 1995 Sweden is a member of the European Union, which means that many new laws that are made in Sweden start out as EU directives. The initially skeptic Swedes have shown a growing support for the union over the last few years. According to the 2009 Eurobarometer, 70 percent of Swedes are optimistic about the future of the union. Sweden is represented by 18 of the 736 members of the European Parliament, and we have ten out of 345 votes in the Council of Ministers. EU elections are held every five years.

Rosenbad (left) is home to the Swedish government.

Sweden has had a king for more than a thousand years, which makes our monarchy one of the oldest in the world?

MONARCHY

Perhaps a little contradictory for such a modern nation, Sweden is also a constitutional monarchy. But although our formal head of state is King Carl XVI Gustaf, the Swedish royal family has long had only representative and ceremonial functions. The people seem to like the glamour that surrounds the royals, though. The monarchy still has widespread public support, so despite the fact that several political parties want Sweden to become a republic, abolishment of the monarchy is not really on the agenda.

By his side, the king has Queen Silvia and their three children—Crown Princess Victoria, Prince Carl Philip and Princess Madeleine. Queen Silvia was born in Germany to the German–Brazilian Sommerlath family. As the story goes, the king and future queen clicked immediately when they first met in Munich in 1972, and they subsequently got married in 1976.

Sweden has been a hereditary kingdom since the days of Gustav Vasa in 1544 and the current successor to the throne is Crown Princess Victoria. It was two years after her birth, in 1979, that Sweden became the first country to make its Act of Succession gender-neutral so as to allow the throne to be passed to the first-born child, whether male or female.

Crown Princess Victoria has become one of Sweden's most important ambassadors, not least through all the attention that her 2010 wedding to commoner Daniel Westling has attracted. Her duties involve supporting the king, replacing him on official engagements and state visits that he is unable to attend. In addition to being involved in international aid work and peace activism, she works with charity through the Crown Princess Victoria's Fund, which supports leisure and recreational activities for children and young people with chronic illnesses or functional disabilities.

Despite her royal upbringing, Crown Princess Victoria is considered to be down to earth and fond of ordinary pastimes like playing golf, skiing and working out. In fact, she met Daniel Westling at the gym where he was the crown princess's personal trainer.

Crown Princess Victoria's laid-back style has helped modernize the image the Swedish royal family.

SWEDEN IN THE WORLD

Located as we are on the Scandinavian Peninsula, off the mainland of Europe, we had the choice to stand on the sidelines. But Swedish companies have almost always looked abroad for a bigger market. We have made a name for ourselves through our active involvement with global issues. Swedish Vikings were certainly out and about, and these days, Swedish tourists are even more eager travelers.

We are not about to stick our head in the sand and ignore global problems like poverty, instability or environmental devastation. Sweden clinched the top spot in the 2009 Commitment to Development Index (CDI), partly because we give 1 percent of our Gross National Income to foreign aid, without any requirement for recipient nations to spend aid money on Swedish goods and services. Sweden is also highly involved in peace mediations and takes part in international peacekeeping missions under the UN. The environmental stance taken by the Swedish government on the international arena also sends a clear message about our commitment to a stable and peaceful world.

Sweden is widely known for its neutrality. We have not been a participant in any war since 1814 and throughout the Cold War remained unaligned in order to make neutrality in the event of war possible. Yet we are currently in command of one of eighteen European Union fast-response units, the Nordic Battle Group. Our neutrality is officially intact, but there is no denying it has been modified to fit a changing world. As a member of the UN and the international community we have long contributed with troops to peace-keeping missions.

If you don't come in contact with Sweden in any other way, chances are you will do business with a Swedish brand like IKEA, H&M or Ericsson. Swedish companies command a disproportionate share of the global market

DID YOU KNOW THAT

both the safety match (Gustaf Erik Pasch in 1844) and dynamite (Alfred Nobel, patented in 1867) are Swedish inventions? Seems like Swedes like to play with fire.

in areas such as telecommunications and biotechnology. The latter is especially interesting due to its high level of international collaborations. Karolinska Institutet, one of Europe's largest and best renowned medical universities, has extensive research partnerships as well as student and staff exchanges with academic institutions around the world. Swedish biotech companies also work closely with foreign academic institutions.

Early on, the limited population of Sweden pushed companies and manufacturers abroad on the look-out for more consumers and a bigger market. They essentially got a head start on globalization. Of course international business is full of mergers and take-overs, companies are traded and sold. But there is an innovative spirit in Sweden that indicates that no matter how many Swedish brands are sold off, there are sure to be new ones coming along. Skype and Spotify are examples of young brands that have recently managed to take the global market by storm.

Two strengths generally associated with Swedish brands are corporate social responsibility (CSR) and environmental know-how. Many Swedish companies have

CSR fits in IKEA's flat packs.

made CSR a part of their corporate culture, and that is now a hot commodity. Swedes know how to make a business successful without corruption while also taking climate change, gender and human rights into account. Over the past few years there have been five Swedish brands on the list of the Global 100 Most Sustainable Corporations in the World, and Sweden has been called a world leader in CSR by organizations such as AccountAbility.

Cultural experiences such as Swedish music, film, design, fashion and gastronomy are marketing themselves with more and more success on the global market. But what most makes Sweden a part of a truly global world is the movement of people. Swedes travel a lot, both for recreation and business. During periods of extreme poverty in the 19th and early 20th century, roughly one third of the population—1.3 million Swedes—migrated to North America for their survival instead. There are almost five million people with Swedish roots in the United States and Canada today.

Meanwhile, 14 percent of the population in Sweden was born in a country other than Sweden. People born in Sweden move abroad and others come back from a period in another country; people born abroad move here and others move back after some years in Sweden. All in all, Sweden definitely feels at home in the world, and we are all glad about the Öresund Bridge which visibly connects us to the European mainland.

INNOVATIONS

A strong culture of innovation has propelled Sweden to the forefront of technological development. The transformation from poor agrarian to highly industrialized country took only a few decades, thanks to a rich supply of raw materials in combination with pioneering inventions like the steam turbine, the ball bearing, the gas-powered beacon and the adjustable wrench.

NOBEL'S WILL

In his last will and testament, Swedish innovator, entrepreneur and industrialist Alfred Nobel (1833–96) decided that the majority of his fortune—accumulated through the registration of 355 patents and the establishment of 90 factories in 20 countries—be set aside for the Nobel Prizes, annual awards to "those who, during the preceding year, shall have conferred the greatest benefit on mankind." An idea that has since overshadowed his own invention of the dynamite in the 1860s.

Every year since 1901, the Nobel Prize has been awarded for achievements in physics, chemistry, physiology or medicine, literature, and for peace. The Sveriges Riksbank Prize in Economic Sciences was not in Nobel's will, but was established in memory of Alfred Nobel in 1968. The award ceremony takes place on December 10, the anniversary of the passing of Nobel, in the Swedish capital of Stockholm, except for the Nobel Peace Prize, which is awarded in Oslo, Norway. It was Nobel who declared that the peace prize should be awarded by a Norwegian committee, which perhaps made more sense back then, as Sweden and Norway were united between 1814 and 1905.

Nobel's original fortune of around SEK 31 million has grown over the years, and since 2001 the prize sum has been SEK 10 million for each of the prizes. Twenty-nine Swedes have so far been awarded the Nobel Prize.

Our long history of ambitious research and development programs seems to indicate an insatiable thirst for knowledge. But it's not only about having clever ideas; it's also about turning them into commercial success. Many Swedish companies are good examples of this.

The founder of telecom company Ericsson, Lars Magnus Ericsson, started his business of developing telegraphs in a small mechanical engineering shop. Subsequently, he contributed to making Stockholm the world's most telephone-dense city in the late 1800s. The firm belief that communication is a basic human need

DID YOU KNOW THAT

in total, since 1901, seven Nobel Prizes in Literature have been
awarded to Swedes over the years?

has been a driving force in Ericsson's development into the global giant it is today.

The IKEA story begins in 1931, when five-year-old Ingvar Kamprad starts selling matches to his neighbors—with a profit. Just twelve years later, he founded a company that he decided to call IKEA, based on his own initials plus the first letters of Elmtaryd and Agunnaryd, the farm and village where he grew up. Six decades later, the company had developed from an entrepreneurial idea in the woods of southern Sweden to a major furniture retail brand present in 40 countries around the world.

Many other everyday items and services, as well as a range of life-saving equipment, are also Swedish innovations. Let's have a closer look at some of them.

Car safety

The three-point seat belt, invented by Vattenfall and developed by Volvo engineer Nils Bohlin, has saved a life every six minutes since its launch in 1959. It is acknowledged as one of the most important car safety innovations ever developed. More recent innovations for safer driving include a new generation of alcolocks and a body tracker that warns night-time drivers if people are walking in front of the car. Both were developed by Autoliv. Over the years, safety-focused Volvo and Saab have pioneered many life-saving innovations.

Koenigsegg's "Flower Power" car

Swedish supercar manufacturer Koenigsegg does not rush development. The Koenigsegg project was launched in 1994, but the first car was only delivered to its customer in 2002. In 2007 they released their CCXR model, which has been equipped with an engine that runs on ethanol—hence its nickname "Flower Power." The world's first environmentally friendly supercar saw the light of day.

Koenigsegg's latest supercar model is called Agera, which is the Swedish verb for "to act."

Gross domestic expenditure on R&D as percentage share of GDP (2007)

The first three-point seat belt was fitted into a Volvo in the late 1950s.

Micro IP

Computer scientist Adam Dunkels has made a name for himself by shrinking the internet protocol (IP). Enabling wireless communication between devices as diverse as satellites, pipelines, electric meters and race car engines, his open-source micro IP is used by hundreds of companies, including NASA, BMW and BBC. Micro IP could also be used in the home: if radiators communicated with a central controller, temperature levels would be fine-tuned and energy consumption reduced.

The zipper

Two woven cotton bands with metal teeth and a pull that can join or separate the teeth—that was Gideon Sundbäck's brilliant idea in 1900. In 1914, his patent was granted, and he had moved to the United States to produce his invention. The appearance of the zipper has not changed over the years, apart from the fact that plastic teeth started replacing the metal teeth in the 1970s.

Skype

In 2003, Swedish entrepreneur Niklas Zennström revolutionized telephone communication. Together with Janus Friis he founded the free internet calling service Skype. In 2009, Skype-to-Skype video and voice calls over the internet accounted for 8 percent of global international calling minutes, which made Skype a leading global internet communications company.

The ball bearing

In 1907, Sven Wingqvist first invented the modern ball bearing, then founded his own company, SKF. The ball bearing turned out to be vital to the development of machine technology, and the Swedish State Railways started using ball bearings for their rolling stock in 1923. SKF has grown to become the almost 45,000-employee worldwide industry it is today.

Black liquor

Swedish company Chemrec has found a way to make use of biomass that would otherwise have been lost, such as tree stumps left in forests or residue from chemical processes at paper mills. A unique black-liquor gasification technology can turn this biomass into fuel, which could potentially replace 25 percent of all petrol and diesel consumption in the country.

The first house on the moon

Imagine a traditional Swedish red cottage being wheeled out of a spacecraft onto the moon and then set down on a suitable spot between the craters. This is the task for a robot being constructed by a group of students at Mälardalen University in Västerås. This solar-powered house-building robot is part of the Luna Resort project, led by artist Mikael Genberg. A prototype has been tested on the Ericsson Globe arena in Stockholm, and—with the help of NASA—the aim is to put the first house on the moon by 2012.

SPOTIFY—A PEACEFUL MUSIC REVOLUTION

In a cultural climate of widespread illegal downloading of music and films, a group of Swedes had a different idea. They invented a web service where music is streamed legally and for free—and Swedish start-up Spotify was born. The company's idea of streaming music online for free may not be completely new, but the technology is unique, and the range of songs available is difficult to match.

Spotify's Chief Technical Officer, Andreas Ehn, and Spotify founder Daniel Ek met while working together for another company. In April 2006, Ek founded Spotify together with entrepreneur Martin Lorentzon, and in August, Ek headhunted computer-savvy Ehn to his new company. Ehn, in turn, helped recruit some of his old study friends from Stockholm's Royal Institute of Technology, KTH.

Today, the small startup has 90 employees and the service is available in a number of countries. Expansion continues and so does the praise: "It blows the doors off of anything on the market and poses a major threat to several music services fighting for attention," the Los Angeles Times commented on Spotify's planned U.S. launch.

(Pirates, also beware of Voddler—another online streaming service in the making, but for film!)

A little red cottage stops on the Ericsson Globe arena in Stockholm on its way to the moon.

Indie star Lykke Li spends a lot of time on tour and feels at home on stage.

Culture and Leisure

Seething with Inspiration

Swedish cultural expressions have literally exploded with creativity and change. Whereas Swedish music used to mean pop and Swedish design used to mean functionality, things cannot be summed up quite as neatly any more. It is less obvious in which directions things are moving, which is also what makes it so much more exciting.

Swedish bands are gaining a foothold in genres as widely different as goth metal and hip hop; our movies no longer stare intensely on the human condition; Swedish art has room for social criticism and the personal; fashion and design may still have one foot in the functional, but the other one is definitively firmly planted in the emotional.

Perhaps the people behind our cultural expressions have simply become more courageous. Or are they increasingly looking abroad for inspiration? Or is the tendency toward a more multicultural society rubbing off on our culture in a more substantial way? It is hard to pinpoint the reasons, but we can see in plain sight that things are a lot different from the days of Bergman and ABBA.

FILM AND STAGE

Sweden cannot and indeed has no ambition to compete with Hollywood, despite one of our more interesting production facilities being dubbed "Trollywood," located in Trollhättan. At the time of writing, however, Swedes are lining up in front of movie theaters to watch films from Sweden more than from any other country (partially a *Millennium* effect). It's unusual, but then again, it's not business as usual for Swedish cinema.

The world of film is changing, and a number of ambitious new Swedish filmmakers are itching to experiment with new techniques and break into genres and markets that have long been outside the Swedish realm. Films such as Tomas Alfredson's adaptation of *Let the Right One In* manage to tickle audiences and critics alike, both in Sweden and abroad. It's no small feat to reinvigorate the vampire genre by successfully blending character-based story with gore and fright. Swedish filmmakers are as interested as Ingmar Bergman and his contemporaries were in describing the

Noomi Rapace as Lisbeth Salander in the Millennium *films.*

human condition, only the perspectives have since changed.

Take Tarik Saleh's futuristic Atmo Media Network drama *Metropia*, which breaks new animation ground. Or non-conformist director Lukas Moodysson, who turned to international-sized budget, stars and shooting locations in his 2009 *Mammoth*. Not even ten million people speak Swedish, which is an issue when raising money for Swedish film; yet for the first time in history Swedish films have had budgets of up to SEK 200 million, indicating a new-born faith in the commercial competitiveness of Swedish cinema. Of course great films do not necessarily require a big coffer, and some directors intentionally choose to make micro productions instead.

Swedish film also has a substantial footing in great documentary and short film production. It is worth keeping an eye on such filmmakers as Jesper Ganslandt, Ruben Östlund and team Åsa Blanck and Johan Palmgren, all with roots in the short and/or documentary genres.

While Swedish productions nowadays attract Hollywood stars, Swedish actors such as Noomi Rapace and Alexander Skarsgård head in the other direction and are well on their way of becoming international stars.

Of course Swedes have things to say on the live stage as well. The Cullberg Ballet has an international reputation, for example, and dance in general is getting more and more attention from Swedish audiences. Stockholm is packed with theaters, from the impressive Dramaten to small independent stages, a number of which are geared specifically towards a young audience.

LITERATURE

Even those who have never read a Swedish author will know at least one of our literary honors, the Nobel Prize awarded by the Swedish Academy. With such a prestigious institution, one might assume that we also have a few literary giants. Sure, both past and present, but the world of books in Sweden also revolves around matters that have little to do with high-brow prizes: the

Illustration from Siv sover vilse (Siv's First Sleep Over) by Pija Lindenbaum.

international best-sellers and books written for a younger audience.

The children's books that take on topics that were recently taboo is probably less of a new trend than a continuation of a literary heritage that started in the 1940s when Astrid Lindgren first wrote about nine-year-old rebellious orphan Pippi Longstocking.

Books such as Bitte Havstad's *Involuntary Siblings* fill an important role. Kids know that parents sometimes divorce, that not all children who live together are related by blood, or have two parents, or two parents of opposite gender. Just as Swedish society has opened up to the idea of alternative family settings since the days of Pippi, so has the need to enable children to read about it.

Moral dilemmas, group pressure and respect for the environment are other common topics. Pija Lindenbaum and Olof and Lena Landström's creations are examples of picture books that explore these topics with a great dose of humor and sensibility. To compete with video games, television and internet, a growing number of fast-paced books—such as Martin Widmark's detective stories—have also flourished.

Of course most detective and crime books are intended for adults. Stieg Larsson's *Millennium* books took the world by storm after his passing. And what a storm it

PUBLIC ART?

Outside the art institutions, an underground creative force is at work. Paintings on tunnel walls, knitted-in lamp posts, bird houses in unexpected places... Provocative, funny and poetic street art is taking place in the urban room, stirring emotions and causing debate. Is this a form of rebellion or is it about changing and decorating the public space? While the Stockholm City Museum organizes guided street-art tours in central Stockholm, many authorities are skeptical about this non-commissioned art in the public space.

was. The books were almost immediately translated into more than forty languages, films were made, and international distributors turned to Sweden for more authors with the same zest. Stieg Larsson followed in the steps of award-winning author Henning Mankell. Their books all have a genuine feel of a brutal reality few of us experience in real life. There are no super-crooks or super-heroes.

Not everything written for grown-ups in Sweden involves murder, though. Jonas Hassen Khemiri is a Swedish author and playwright on the brink of international importance. His plays and books often deal with identity, race and language. Of the classics, perhaps only August Strindberg—who left a decided mark on modern theater—is widely remembered abroad. But Sweden produces great authors in everything from strict literary genres to pop fiction, with unique strengths in children's literature, crime novels and, if the success of Johan Ajvide Lindqvist's books is any indication, also horror novels with a human touch. Apparently, Swedish books are doing frighteningly well.

ART

Swedish art is a wide open field. In a climate where nothing is sacred and a variety of new media are available, social criticism rubs shoulders with the personal and poetic. Authenticity is no longer relevant, which often makes art appear as a mix of reality, distance and distortion.

More and more artists use art as a meeting place. Music, choreography, and old and new media can come together and create something new. Nathalie Djurberg, for example, made her installation *The Experiment* by combining her "claymation" (clay-animated) short films with gigantic, sculpted clay flowers and music. Her work shows that the narrative has returned to the Swedish art scene, sometimes expressed in some rather

bizarre stories. Djurberg questions society's conventions through films that may look naïve at first glance, but are in fact very violent and erotic, spiced with ironic humor.

Video is a predominant medium in Sweden, and a remarkably large part of the video artists are women. Ann-Sofi Sidén has been investigating the human psyche through a mix of journalism, feature films and scientific studies since the early 1990s. For her, the video medium serves to capture moments of reality and expose details of people's body language and facial expressions.

Henrik Håkansson turns his investigative eye on nature. A traditional theme in Swedish art, love of nature, was especially visible in the works of late 19th-century artists such as Anders Zorn, Carl Larsson and Bruno Liljefors. Håkansson takes nature into the 21st-century art by examining it in a new way. Using technology and music, he creates a kind of "bio-aesthetics" where the communication between culture and nature is central.

So, does figurative art still fit on the Swedish scene? Yes, artists like critically acclaimed Gunnel Wåhlstrand seem to prove that. She meticulously recreates old family photos in the shape of giant, extremely realistic paintings using an ink-wash technique. While telling a very personal story, Wåhlstrand takes craftsmanship to new heights through her precise and excruciatingly time-consuming work.

MUSIC

In Sweden, music is never far away from everyday life. We sing, simple as that. Sweden is also one of the biggest export nations of music in the world, and the biggest by far in terms of per capita. Listeners don't necessarily know that what they are moving to on the dance floor, hearing on the radio or in the TV commercial, or for that matter downloading from the internet, is actually

Nathalie Djurberg makes her mark with gigantic clay creations.

DID YOU KNOW THAT

there is a Swedish string instrument called nyckelharpa *used widely in our folk music?*
Check out Hedningarna ("The Heathens") for a sample of the sound.

Swedish. Even most Swedes don't know—there is too much to keep up with.

There are foreign bloggers who write about nothing but Swedish music, and it's a full-time job. In addition to the acts that break through internationally, there are Swedish producers and songwriters behind international stars and Swedish directors behind their music videos.

If you are wondering about the reason behind our success, look to the highest number of per capita choirs in the world, or why not, the deeply rooted sing-along culture or the festive singing that takes place at parties during Midsummer, Christmas or an autumn crawfish party. There is also a supportive cultural policy that allows for smaller events where newcomers can work out their act, as well as municipal music schools that allow anyone with an interest to experiment with music from an early age.

With ABBA, Sweden pretty much had one band, one identity, at least as far as the world knew. They were blond, beautiful, and a little bit odd. They were Sweden. It is a little more

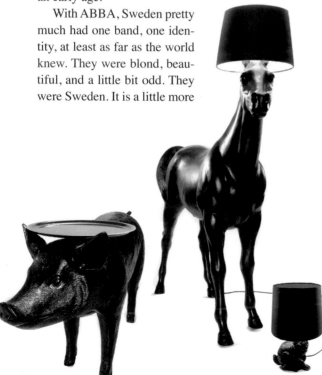

confusing now, but also more exciting, with successful performers and bands in almost any category you can think of, from jazz to doom metal. Following the development of the country at large, Swedish music export has become less homogenous.

The deep roots of Swedish jazz dig into both their American counterpart and Swedish folk. The tragic passing of the front man of the Esbjörn Svenson Trio (E.S.T.) in 2008 in no way meant the end of Swedish jazz. Sweden has also long been a hotbed of heavy metal and its subgenres, launching the careers of some of the most innovative metal bands. There are over a hundred internationally viable heavier rock bands in Sweden.

There are success stories to be told in other genres too: classical, reggae, hip hop, to mention a few, but perhaps pop and indie attracts the most attention and is where the most Swedish of sounds can be found, if there is such a thing at all. Robyn, Lykke Li, Shout Out Louds, Andreas Tilliander… have we forgotten anyone? Of course we have. More and more artists realize that if they want to support themselves with their music, their Swedish audiences are not big enough. Others just find themselves in the midst of the international limelight, uncertain just how they got there.

DESIGN AND CRAFT

Diversity and blurred boundaries. That pretty much sums up the contemporary Swedish design scene. A new generation of designers want to tell a story through their objects, not simply create useful things. As function meets emotion, the creative range becomes wider than ever and the clean and simple IKEA style gets competition.

Many designers have adopted a cross-disciplinary approach to their work—art, craft and design are often mixed and matched. Drawing inspiration from

Sami craft as well as urban life, Monica Förster renews familiar shapes by using unexpected materials and new techniques in her minimalist furniture and objects. She believes that producing high-quality design is an effective countermeasure against the culture of consumption.

An investigative approach is found in the work of Front. Cooperating from first ideas to final product, this tight-knit design team often lets external factors decide the shape. In their Design by Animals collection, the gnawing of rats has created a wallpaper pattern, and their Flower Lamp changes shape depending on how much energy a household uses. Front's innovative style has also made its way into furniture giant IKEA's PS 2009 collection.

Perhaps inspired by the flurry of new creativity around them, traditional Swedish glassworks Kosta Boda is also treading new ground. By taking on board glass artist Åsa Jungnelius with her over-sized goblets and giant glass lipsticks, they have incorporated a style that is more fun than functional, more expressive than exclusive. But the true master of blending genres is perhaps craftswoman and designer Zandra Ahl. When she lets fine art interact with popular culture and modern consumerism, the result is an overwhelmingly "kitschy" style that challenges traditional aesthetics.

Ahl's work is a far cry from the previously predominant functionalism. Ever since the breakthrough of functionalism at the Stockholm Exhibition of 1930, form has more or less been dictated by function in Sweden. The general perception is still that "Swedish design" refers to pure lines, blond wood and user-friendliness. Admittedly, IKEA may have something to do with this, but it all started with the 1919 pamphlet *Better Things for Everyday Life* written by Swedish art historian Gregor Paulsson. He pointed out the need for making aesthetic objects more widely available, a statement that had an

Animals are a recurring theme in Front's design.

enormous impact on Swedish design for most of the 20th century. Paulsson's idea of democratic, non-elitist design is still valid, and it is striking what an important role design plays in Swedes' everyday life.

Furniture designer and architect Bruno Mathsson's modernism from the 1930s and 1940s was groundbreaking at the time and put Sweden on the international design map—and still does, in fact. But his "Swedish Modern" aesthetics is now challenged by a more emotional style, where design can be a statement and the notion of what is beautiful is being re-evaluated.

FASHION

Swedish fashion is changing. Just like in the design arena as a whole, many fashion designers have moved on from the long-established focus on function. While H&M still spreads affordable Swedish style around the globe, a number of cutting-edge designers are leading the way toward a more individual creative expression.

Sandra Backlund has knitted her way onto the international catwalk in a style far removed from the traditionally so pragmatic Swedish approach. Extravagant and expressive, her thick and chunky woolly creations are the result of true craftsmanship. She experiments with the body's natural silhouette and describes her own style as "a combination of science fiction and sheltered, warm pieces of fantasy." A first prize at the fashion festival in French Hyères in 2007 was Backlund's ticket to the international fashion stage.

An equally craftsman-like approach is found in the studio of Rickard Lindqvist, but his expression is completely different. Using traditional tailoring techniques, he creates slightly anarchistic versions of classic clothing. He is very interested in pattern construction, and feels that there is an important aesthetic in that phase as well. Currently pursuing a PhD at the Swedish School

Anna von Schewen has won the Bruno Mathsson Award for her furniture design.

Top ten fastest growing Swedish fashion brands, 2007 compared to 2006

1. WEEKDAY BRANDS +349%

2. ODD MOLLY +139%

3. RNB, RETAIL AND BRANDS +126%

4. ZARA SVERIGE +79%

5. GINA TRICOT +69%

6. WEEKDAY RETAIL +66%

7. PEKAVE GRUPPEN +62%

8. BJÖRN BORG +53%

9. VAGABOND BUTIKER +52%

10. BLÅKLÄDER +50%

One of Sandra Backlund's knitted wonders.

of Textiles in Borås, Lindqvist is also proof of the fact that fashion has been granted academic status. In 2006 the Centre for Fashion Studies was established at Stockholm University, along with Sweden's first professorship in fashion studies.

While the Swedish fashion scene is bursting with creativity, many designers are struggling to transform their talent into a viable business. But the three sisters behind the brand Minimarket, Sofie, Pernilla and Jennifer Elvestedt, have found their recipe for success. They make collections characterized by feminine shapes with masculine influences, often in strong colors, and in their own words, they "aim to complete other Swedish brands rather than compete with them." But it is clear that they have become quite a commercial success, with their garments being sold in shops all around the world.

An ecological consciousness is also starting to reach the world of fashion. Brands like Nudie, Camilla Norrback and Julian Red are striving for increased environmental and ethical awareness in the fashion world, and have started to show that eco can also be chic. When you buy new jeans, do you consider the fact that the equivalent of a year's minimum consumption of water is used in the production process in a world where a billion people lack access to clean water? Dem Collective has found a better way, which the story to the right shows.

What has been called "the Swedish fashion miracle" actually started in the denim world, with brands like Acne, Nudie and WESC, that have all achieved global success. One of the followers, Cheap Monday, also made a name for itself very quickly and was sold to H&M in 2008 for SEK 500 million.

The interest in fashion among Swedes has exploded over the last decade. H&M's affordable yet trendy clothes are surely one explanation for this, but it also has

to do with the fact that the economic situation has improved for the majority of Swedes. A reaction against the culture of consumerism, however, is the growing second hand market for fashion. Last year's haute couture may be this year's street wear.

ZANDRA'S STORY

Zandra Ahl started questioning the old design ideals by bringing kitsch into the establishment. She uses strong colors and mass-produced materials in her craft work. Already during her studies at the University College of Arts, Crafts and Design in Stockholm, she ignored the prevailing design "rules" and went her own way. Ahl's very personal style—seductive and disturbing at the same time—is inspired by feminism and postmodernism, and her work is a comment on the material culture we live in and the elitism that surrounds us.

DEM COLLECTIVE

Karin Stenmar once needed to order 50 T-shirts for a jazz club she was working at. A supplier offered T-shirts for SEK 9.90 each, including print. Karin reacted: at such a low price, the T-shirts couldn't have been produced under acceptable social and environmental conditions.

Finding no better alternatives, Karin and her friend Annika Axelsson, who was at the time in Sri Lanka on a research project, decided to start their own ethically conscious production of garments from ecological cotton—in Sri Lanka. So, in 2004, the brand Dem Collective was born.

Karin's and Annika's social entrepreneurship has turned into a success story. With a continually growing turnover, the company now has offices in Gothenburg and Stockholm, factories in Sri Lanka and India, and is involved in a cooperation project in Egypt. And Dem Collective's clothes are not only environmentally friendly and fairly produced; they are also considered well designed and of high quality.

Nudie jeans brand steps up to the ecological challenge.

DID YOU KNOW THAT

Sweden's ice-hockey team Tre Kronor ("Three Crowns") was the first in history to win the gold in both the Olympic Games and the world championships in the same year (2006)? They did not do as well in the 2010 Olympics.

SPORTS

Sweden is widely perceived as a nation that takes care of its citizens from the cradle to the grave. But we also take care of ourselves as individuals. Swedes love to stay healthy, and are, according to several recent studies, among some of the healthiest and longest-living people in the world. We are a nation of amateur athletes and physical exercise enthusiasts. It's a social movement of sorts.

One of the underlying reasons for this (the other being the surrounding nature that beckons us outside) actually lies in our long history of political involvement by ordinary people through "popular movements"—in this case the sports movement rather than unions, the women's movement, or the temperance movement. Through these movements, citizens have long worked for everyone's equal chance to participate in society.

These sports organizations still engage a lot of people from all social classes and ages, though a growing number of people choose more loosely organized sports such as adventure sports, or simply work out at the gym. The breadth and popular support enjoyed by the Swedish sports movement also helps explain Sweden's disproportional success in international sports events in relation to its population.

We have somehow managed to get to where we are without being very competitive. How very Swedish of us. Currently we are keeping our eyes on Zlatan Ibrahimovic (soccer), Charlotte Kalla (cross-country skiing), Robin Söderling (tennis), Nicklas Bäckström (ice hockey) and Sarah Sjöström (swimming).

Anti-doping is of importance to Sweden. A society with widespread opposition against recreational drugs is obviously against doping. While a major drug scandal in Swedish sport is not impossible, it remains unlikely. Swedish scientists hold a leading position in such research as the discovery of blood doping and testosterone misuse.

TRADITIONS

Sweden is a secular society today. But religion still plays an important role, since many of our traditions have religious roots. And we do like to celebrate, so even if we may have forgotten the origins of certain customs, we still observe them.

Religions and traditions from other parts of the world are also enriching our country, Islam's Ramadan being one example. With an estimated 400,000 Muslims in Sweden, this month of fasting doesn't go unnoticed in Swedish society. But when different traditions meet and blend, Swedes also hold on to old customs. Perhaps keeping one foot in history adds a much needed feeling of continuity to our lives, a sense of belonging.

Many Swedish traditions are closely linked to the changing seasons. While winter celebrations demand a ridiculous amount of lit candles, outdoor activities of some sort are a must at summer parties. Let us give you a snapshot of the Swedish year in celebrations, expanding on a selected few: Midsummer, the crayfish party, Lucia and Christmas.

Midsummer

June: Schools are out and nature has burst into life. It seems like the sun never sets. In fact, in the north of Sweden it doesn't, and in the south only for an hour or two. This calls for celebration! Let's round up friends and family for the most Swedish of our traditions: Midsummer.

The summer solstice is the reason why we celebrate Midsummer. Ever since pagan times, Swedes have been eager to feast through the longest day of the year, on or around June 21. Since the 1950s we have, for practical reasons, celebrated Midsummer on Midsummer Eve, which is always on a Friday between June 19 and June 25.

If you want solitude on Midsummer, stay in the city. This weekend there is an exodus from the cities to the country, where revelers meet up with friends and family.

A few more or less compulsory rituals precede the midsummer meal:

Picking wild flowers—both for the wreath that you will be wearing on your head and for the maypole, or rather, midsummer pole.

Dressing the midsummer pole in leaves and flowers.

Raising the midsummer pole somewhere convenient, where there is dancing space around it.

Time for lunch! Typically, a table is set outside, decorated with a nice cloth and maybe some flowers left over from the wreath and pole. Normally, the same table will have to be moved inside due to sudden rain showers. We often joke that Midsummer is cursed, because it is quite often accompanied by damp and fairly cold weather. Of course, the more experienced hostesses and hosts don't take any chances; they set up a tent in advance, and ask their guests to wear something warm.

The food on the table is fairly basic: different varieties of pickled herring, new potatoes with dill and sour cream. Fresh strawberries with whipped cream or strawberry cake often follow. Most adults like to wash down the herring with schnapps (a shot of alcohol), usually preceded by a short, often quite silly schnapps song, of which there are plenty, passed on from generation to generation. The Swedish schnapps is distilled from grain or potato and is often flavored, but never sweet.

When people are fed and happy, the dancing can begin. Adults and children alike form a circle around the midsummer pole and dance to traditional songs. The actual dancing is more or less a matter of moving in one direction, so not too complicated. Many towns and villages arrange public midsummer dancing, where

Zlatan "Ibra" Ibrahimovic adds a little flair before netting the ball.

JANUARY
Epiphany
6
Baltsar

FEBRUARY
Shrove Tuesday
16
Julie

APRIL
Easter Day
4
SUNDAY
Marianne   Marlene

AUGUST
Crayfish Party Premiere
4
WEDNE
Arne

APRIL
Walpurgis
Night
30

JUNE
National Day
6
SUNDAY
Gustav   Gösta

JUNE
Midsummer Eve
25
FRIDAY
Rakel

MAY
Ascension Day
13
THURSDAY
nea   Linn

NOVEMBER
Martin Goose
Day
10
artina

OCTOBER
Halloween
31
SUNDAY
Edit   Edgar

AUGUST
Fermented Herring
Party Premiere
19
THURSDAY
Magnus   Måns

DECEMBER
Lucia
13

NOVEMBER
All Saints Day
6
SATURDAY
Gustav Adolf

DECEMBER
Christmas Eve
24
FRIDAY
Eva

NOVEMBER
Advent Sunday
28
SUNDAY
Malte

DECEMBER
New Year's Eve
31
FRIDAY
Sylvester

*Swedes have lots of celebrations
to look forward to every year.
When we talk about "red days,"
we refer to the national holidays
marked red in the calendar.*

a group of folk musicians accompany the dancing crowd.

As it never really gets dark on Midsummer, the party can go on for hours on end. Eventually, the mist starts dancing across the fields, and it may, after all, be time for bed.

The crayfish party

August: Ideally, nights are now warm and tender and boiled crayfish are heaped onto each and every table. This previously very exclusive delicacy can nowadays be bought any time of the year, but most Swedes save the crayfish slurping for the traditional premiere in August. The concept is easy: get together with a few friends, eat lots of crayfish, drink some beer and schnapps, and top it all off with some singing.

Similarly to Midsummer, the crayfish party preferably takes place outdoors. In this case, however, this also has a practical reason: eating crayfish is a messy business, and eating them indoors can leave a long-lasting smell. Who wants to wake up in the smell of old fish? For the same practical reason, decorations tend to be of paper— cloths, plates, napkins and lanterns. For the more orthodox, bibs and silly paper hats can also be added to the list. Cleaning up is easy: just throw everything into a garbage bag.

The crayfish are fished out of lakes and rivers, or the sea. Swedes tend to have a preference for either sweetwater or saltwater crayfish depending on whether we are from the east coast or the west coast. The little creatures are boiled with lots of dill, and sometimes a dash of beer. Landed on our plates, they are shelled, sucked and devoured. The typically accompanying schnapps comes, just like at the Midsummer party, with some singing.

Generally we pick up already boiled and packaged crayfish from the supermarket fridge or freezer. And to help us make the right choice there, many newspapers publish annual crayfish tests, where they rate different brands from different countries. Opinions range from "tastes like mud" to "perfect saltiness and just the right amount of dill," and it doesn't take long for the winning crayfish to sell out.

The most common crayfish in Sweden is the imported signal crayfish, native to the western United States. Unfortunately, it brought the crayfish plague with it, so the European crayfish or "noble crayfish," has become an endangered species. Although a serious ecological problem, Swedes in general don't seem too worried about this. There are plenty more fish in the sea, as the saying goes… As long as we get served some sort of crayfish at the August feast, we are happy as clams at high tide.

Lucia and Christmas

December: If we are lucky, snow has fallen to brighten up the quickly darkening nights, creating that special Christmas feeling. Maybe Christmas is just as commercial in Sweden as anywhere else, but it's also a

Lucia processions bring light.

LEGENDARY LUCIA

St Lucia is surrounded by many legends—was she St Lucia of Syracuse or maybe Adam's first wife? Her name may be associated with both lux (light) and Lucifer (the devil). In the old calendar, Lucia night was the longest night of the year. Back then, most Swedes seemed to agree that it was a dangerous night, when animals could speak and supernatural beings were lurking in the dark. Many preferred to stay awake through the night. In fact, some young people still observe the tradition of Lucia wake—but normally just as an excuse for an all-night party.

━━━━━━━━━━━━━━━━━━━━━━

time when we bring out our hand-crafted decorations, fill our homes with candlelight, and go back to our grandmother's recipes to bake ginger snaps and saffron buns.

Starting on the first of Advent, four Sundays before Christmas, December is party time. Friends and neighbors invite each other over for sweet mulled wine and offices have Christmas parties. As secular as Swedes may be, even we admit that the Christmas season and all its traditions are sacred to us.

December 13 is Lucia Day. In preschools all over the country, little feet are shuffling and white nightgowns are flapping, making candle lights flicker. The children of the annual Lucia procession sing well-known, traditional songs of Lucia and Christmas in front of immensely proud parents.

Most girls—and the occasional boy—want the leading part of Lucia, and in preschool everyone who wants it, gets it. Lucia wears a wreath with electric candles on her head and a red ribbon around her waist. Traditionally, the other girls are Lucia's handmaidens, carrying candles in their hands instead. Most boys are little Santas dressed in red, star boys in white gowns with paper cones on their heads and stars on sticks in their hands, or gingerbread men.

As the children grow older, there is only room for one Lucia, and competition is fierce. Every passing year also makes it increasingly difficult to recruit star boys, as they become more and more reluctant to wear a girly night gown.

Eleven days later is Christmas Eve. In our book, December 24 is the big day of Santa Claus and Christmas presents, which most Swedes like to celebrate with their loved ones. Christmas Day and the day after are also holidays in the Swedish calendar, and when possible, we prefer to also take the days between Christmas and New Year off, giving us a nice, long and relaxing vacation.

A mouth-watering Christmas smorgasbord of pickled herring, meatballs, Christmas ham and much, much more is often served at lunch time on December 24. At 3 p.m., it's "Donald Duck" time. Funny as it may sound, Swedes, young and old, gather in front of the TV to watch Christmas-theme Disney cartoons, the decorated Christmas tree glittering in the background. This program has been an indispensable part of the celebrations ever since the 1960s. Then: a sudden knock on the door. Santa Claus is here! Eager children rip open their Christmas presents and can finally start playing with their new toys. Remember Jesus, anyone?

GASTRONOMY

The Swedish food landscape has changed over the last decade. The Swedish chef, once only known as a character in *The Muppet Show*, is no longer a laughing matter. Through top-class cooking and innovative use of raw materials, the Swedish chef has won the world's recognition, taking home gold medals at the culinary Olympic Games, as well as several medals at the un-

THE NORDIC DIET

According to recent research, Swedes' typical diet of fatty fish, cabbage, root vegetables and berries is among the healthiest in the world. Based on food that is easily grown and produced in colder climates, this so-called Nordic diet is both cheap and environmentally friendly to produce and consume for people in northern Europe. So the Mediterranean diet had better look out—here comes the swede!

━━━━━━━━━━━━━━━━━━━━━━

official world championship, the Bocuse d'Or. And with gourmet restaurants opening their doors all over the country, Sweden has turned into one of the haute-cuisine hot spots in Europe.

But to be honest, it's not all about the chefs. Our local raw materials also contribute to Sweden's culinary success. Fresh catches and harvests from lakes, forests, mountains and meadows inspire creativity and make for delicious, ecological dishes. This is true for restaurants and private homes alike. Our unique right of public access grants us the right to pick wild strawberries, chanterelles and other goodies we may find in nature, so it's easy as pie for anyone to make a gourmet meal at home—all for free.

Historically, Swedish food culture was based on the need to store food. This is why fresh berries used to be cooked into jam, vegetables pickled, mushrooms dried, and meat and fish smoked, salted, fermented, marinated… Many young chefs use traditional cooking as their starting point, add a twist and—presto—a new gastronomic creation is born.

We have taken the liberty of using three recipes from Ethiopian-born Swedish chef Marcus Samuelsson as examples of the new Swedish cuisine. Why don't you try them yourself?

≫→

Christmas-decorated amusement park Liseberg lights up Gothenburg.

MARCUS SAMUELSSON

Marcus Samuelsson was born in Addis Ababa in Ethiopia in 1970, and adopted by Swedish parents at the age of three. Set on becoming a chef early on in life, Samuelsson had his breakthrough as chef for well-reputed New York restaurant Aquavit in the mid-1990s with his Scandinavian cooking. Today, he is involved in several restaurants, among them the Swedish Aquavit restaurant in Stockholm, is a guest professor at Umeå University School of Restaurant and Culinary Arts, and has written several inspiring cook books. Samuelsson was also chosen as guest chef for U.S. President Barack Obama's first official state dinner.

Pickled herring with bean and potato salad

Having served as staple food in Sweden for centuries, even millennia, herring still has a central place on our smorgasbord. Most Swedes cannot imagine Midsummer or Christmas celebrations without it. And it is still usually served the old, pickled way. This is a recipe for the more Baltic-style herring, which is first fried then pickled, served with new accessories.

SERVES 4
INGREDIENTS

4 fillets of fried pickled herring*
3 ½ oz/1 dl large white beans, soaked overnight and boiled, or canned
8 potatoes, boiled and cut into pieces
2 small onions, chopped
3 cloves of garlic, sliced
2 tbs almond, blanched and chopped
3 spring onions, chopped
juice of 1½ lemon
3 tbs ground sumac
4 tbs dill, chopped
3 tbs olive oil
butter
chili, salt and pepper

PREPARATION

1. Fry the almond in butter together with the onions and the garlic. When browned, add sumac (a Middle Eastern spice with a lemony flavor) and stir.

2. Mix the beans and potatoes with lemon juice and olive oil. Season with chili, salt and pepper. Slowly stir in spring onions, dill and the almonds. Mix carefully and season again.

3. Serve the spicy salad with fried pickled herring. Top off with a sprig of dill.

*In Sweden, fried pickled herring can be bought in many supermarkets, but here is a quick guide to how you can prepare it yourself:

1. Roll fresh, cleaned herring in rye flour, salt and white pepper, and fry it in butter.

2. Mix one part distilled white vinegar (12%), two parts sugar and three parts water in a pot, and boil for a few minutes together with some sliced onion and carrot and a teaspoon of whole allspice.

3. Pickle the fried fish in the cooled sauce.

Reindeer meatballs with glazed garlic confit and red cabbage

Swedes have eaten reindeer meat since at least the ninth century B.C. Back then, it was all about hunting, now it's a proper industry. More than 200,000 reindeer are herded by around 4,500 reindeer owners in the northern third of Sweden. Reindeer husbandry is an old Sami right, and forms the basis of their culture. This recipe uses reindeer meat to give a new touch to traditional Swedish meatballs.

SERVES 4
INGREDIENTS

8 pieces of reindeer sirloin, 1 ½ tbs/20 g each

Meatball mix:
1 small red onion, finely chopped
2 tbs breadcrumbs
1¾ oz/0.5 dl cream
2 eggs
¾ lb/300 g ground beef and pork meat
salt and freshly ground pepper
butter, olive oil

Honey-glazed garlic confit:
4 garlics, in cloves and peeled
4 fresh thyme sprigs
3 ½ oz/1 dl balsamic vinegar
3 ½ oz/1 dl honey
1 cinnamon stick
butter
salt and freshly ground pepper

Spicy red cabbage:
½ head of red cabbage, finely chopped
1 tsp garam masala
2 small red onions, chopped
4 oz/1.25 dl liquid honey
3 ½ oz/1 dl port
fresh thyme
2 tbs demerara sugar
2 cinnamon sticks
salt and freshly ground pepper
oil

PREPARATION

Reindeer meatballs:
1. Sauté the onion in butter and leave to cool.

2. Mix breadcrumbs and cream in a bowl and let it soak for a few minutes. Add first eggs, then onion and the ground meat. Season with salt and pepper.

3. Cut the reindeer meat into cubes. Envelope each reindeer cube in ground meat to form eight balls. (If there is time, let the meatballs rest in the fridge for 20 minutes.)

4. Fry the meatballs in oil and butter on medium heat until golden brown, for around 7–8 minutes. Lift them out of the pan and keep them warm.

Honey-glazed garlic confit:
Sauté the garlic cloves in a pan. Add vinegar, honey, thyme and cinnamon. Boil on medium heat for around 20 minutes. Stir in a knob of butter and season with salt and pepper.

Not only does this give you beautiful, glazed garlic cloves, it is also the perfect base for a sauce.

Spicy red cabbage:
Pour some oil into a large saucepan. Add the red cabbage, garam masala, red onion, honey, salt, pepper, port, thyme, sugar and cinnamon. Simmer on low heat for around 40 minutes.

The meatballs can be served out of the frying pan, with cabbage and sauce on the side.

If you can't get hold of reindeer meet, just exclude it from the recipe and do "normal" meatballs with only minced meat. The traditional Swedish way of serving meatballs is with mashed potatoes and lingonberry jam.

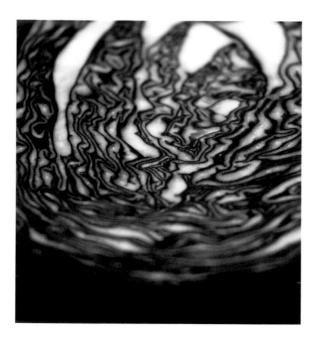

Cloudberry soufflé

The sub-Arctic cloudberry can withstand cold temperatures down to well below −40°F (−40°C) and thrives in bogs, marshes and wet meadows as it needs humidity. They grow all over the country, but are more common in the north. Despite the fact that cloudberries are very healthy—rich in omega-3 fatty acids, vitamins and antioxidants—the recipe below is nevertheless a delicious treat after a nice meal.

SERVES 4
INGREDIENTS

juice of 1 lime
2 tsp water
3 ½ oz/1 dl sugar
1 vanilla pod
5 egg whites
3 oz/1 dl cloudberries
4 soufflé ramekins
butter and sugar for the ramekins

PREPARATION

1. Heat the oven to 390°F/200°C.

2. Mix lime juice, water and sugar in a saucepan. Cut the vanilla pod lengthwise and scrape the seeds into the saucepan. Bring to the boil, and boil until the sugar has melted. Then pass the mix through a sieve.

3. Whisk the egg whites until stiff, using a mixer. Add the sugar syrup carefully while still whisking. Keep whisking for around 5 minutes.

Grown wild and hand picked, cloudberries are a treasured find—whether in the forest or on the kitchen table.

4. Slowly add the cloudberries. Be sure to save some for garnish.

5. Brush the soufflé ramekins—ovenproof coffee cups may be used—with some melted butter and coat them with sugar. Ladle the mix into the ramekins and bake in the oven for 7 minutes.

6. Garnish with cloudberries.

If you are not lucky enough to be in cloudberry land, you can also use the ubiquitous raspberry.

This apple dessert helped the Swedish national team win the bronze medal at the Culinary Olympics 2008.

Food and Drinks

Smör *Butter*
Ost *Cheese*
Bröd *Bread*
Knäckebröd *Crispbread*
Kött *Meat*
Fisk *Fish*
Skaldjur *Shellfish*
Kyckling *Chicken*
Vegetariskt *Vegetarian*
Köttbullar och lingonsylt *Meatballs and lingonberry jam*
En dagens, tack! *Today's special, please (mostly lunch time)*
Vatten *Water*
Mjölk *Milk*
Lättöl *Low-alcohol beer (a maximum of 2.25% alcohol by volume, common in Sweden)*
En stor stark *A lager beer ("a big strong")*
Ett glas rött/vitt *A glass of red/white wine*
Kaffe på maten *Coffee after dinner*

Feelings

Jag gillar dig *I like you*
Jag älskar dig *I love you*
Jag hatar dig *I hate you*
Jag är ledsen *I'm sorry/I'm sad (depending on the context)*
Förlåt! *I'm sorry/Forgive me*

Numerals

0 Noll	6 Sex
1 Ett	7 Sju
2 Två	8 Åtta
3 Tre	9 Nio
4 Fyra	10 Tio
5 Fem	

Greetings and Courtesies

Hej! *Hello*
Tjena! *Hi (informal)*
Talar du engelska? *Do you speak English?*
Hur mår du? *How are you? (neutral)*
Hur står det till? *How are you? (formal)*
Hur är läget? *What's up? (informal)*
Bara bra, tack. Och du? *I'm fine, thanks. And you?*
Trevligt att träffas *Pleased to meet you*
Hejdå! *Bye-bye*

God morgon! *Good morning*
God natt! *Good night*
Tack! *Thank you/Please (depending on the context)*
Varsågod! *Here you go/Please/You're welcome (depending on the context)*
Ursäkta mig! *Excuse me*
Ursäkta mig, var ligger toaletten? *Excuse me, where is the restroom/toilet?*

Typically Swedish

Fika *Coffee break (including the socializing that goes with it)*
Påtår *A refill of coffee (often included)*
Glögg *The Swedish version of mulled wine*
Lagom *Just right; not too little, not too much*
Nja (nej + ja) *No and yes*
Smörgåsbord *Smorgasbord*
Ombudsman *Ombudsman (!)*
Sambo *Someone who lives together with his/her partner without being married (short for samboende)*
Särbo *Someone who is in a long-term relationship but does not live together with his/her partner*
Älg *Moose (elk)*

On the Web

Tyda.se: Online dictionary
Si.se/studyswedish: Tutored web course in Swedish

SWEDISH LANGUAGE

Swedish is a North Germanic language, spoken by almost ten million people both in and outside of Sweden, especially in Finland. Originally, Swedish comes from Old Norse, the common language in Scandinavia during the Viking Era. Norwegians, Danes and Swedes normally understand each other, but our Eastern neighbors in Finland speak a completely different language with roots in the so-called Uralic languages.

The Swedish alphabet is a 29-letter alphabet, using the basic 26-letter Latin alphabet plus the three additional letters Å, Ä and Ö. There are many words of German, French and, especially lately, English origin in the Swedish language, but the words are often transcribed to the Swedish spelling system.

Swedish is officially the main language of Sweden—but only since July 1, 2009, when a new language law was implemented. Until then, the Swedish language had no official status in law strangely enough, despite being used in local and national government and most of the educational system. The new law says that, for example, safety instructions and product information must be available in Swedish. And the language used in schools should normally be Swedish.

The new law also promotes and protects Sweden's five national minority languages: Finnish, all Sami dialects, Torne Valley Finnish (Meänkieli), Romani Chib and Yiddish. Children whose parents belong to a national minority are entitled to learn that language even if it may not be their mother tongue. The Swedish sign language has the same status as the minority languages in the law, and deaf or hearing-impaired children and their families also have a right to learn the language.

The Swedish language law also covers all other mother tongues spoken in Sweden, about 150 different ones. It states that everyone is entitled to use their mother tongue, so it cannot be forbidden in the workplace, for example. The Swedish Education Act determines the right for children of immigrant parents to have Mother Tongue Studies as a school subject.

DID YOU KNOW THAT the letter "å" (sounds like the "o" in "for") came into the Swedish language when the New Testament was printed in 1526? The printer decided to create a new letter by putting a small "o" above the "a," and the letter has been used ever since. "Ä" and "ö" were created similarly, by writing an "e" above "a" and "o," respectively.

History

From Ice Age to IT Age

The year: 110,000 B.C. It is very, very cold in Sweden and the country is covered in ice. At the beginning of the Stone Age (12,000–1700 B.C.), the ice has receded enough to let the first immigrants arrive and settle in Sweden. Dressed in animal skin, they use their stone weapons to hunt, reindeer being their main prey.

The Bronze Age (1700–500 B.C.) starts out with a climate that is actually warmer than today. Those who can afford it start to use better tools and weapons made of bronze, an obvious improvement to their lives.

The Iron Age (500 B.C.–1050 A.D.) brings our first written language, the runic script, an adaptation of Greek and Roman letters. It is discovered that iron makes for both better and cheaper tools and weapons than bronze.

Enter the Vikings. The period between 700 and 1050 A.D. is marked by their expeditions and raids around Europe, especially eastwards. Trouble around the Mediterranean has brought more trade to the north and Swedes start to make use of their shipbuilding skills. The fact that Vikings are free men as opposed to those who stay to farm the land and the slaves, probably makes it easy to recruit people to the "expeditions" that are sometimes peaceful trade journeys, sometimes brutal raids where robbery is the only currency.

Some highlights from the thousand years that follows, until today, are illustrated in the following timeline.

Husaby kyrka, where Olof Skötkonung was baptized.

Birger Jarl

The University of Uppsala was founded in 1477— the first university in Scandinavia.

The Stockholm Bloodbath.

Gustav Vasa

1008

Around 1008: Olof Skötkonung becomes Sweden's first Christian king, and the first to rule the first version of the kingdom of Sweden (Svea Rike, later Sverige).

1155

1050–1500:
The Middle Ages

1155: Finland is joined to the Swedish realm, through a crusade.

1248–1266: Statesman Birger Jarl introduces the first national laws concerning the protection of women, the home, churches and the court.

1349

1349: The Black Death kills one-third of the Swedish-Finnish population, and a long period of economic decline follows.

1391

End of the 1300s: Sweden-Finland has about 650,000 inhabitants.

1391: Saint Birgitta or Bridget, founder of the Brigittine Order, was canonized in Rome. An unusually powerful woman for her time, she made her voice heard among kings and clergy.

1520

1520: The Stockholm Bloodbath. Kristian II "the Tyrant" executes 100 people.

1521

1521–1611:
The Vasa Period

1523: Gustav Vasa becomes king. He continues the centralization of power and Sweden becomes a unified state. The population increases.

The Battle of Poltava.

1668

1668: The world's oldest still existing national bank, today's Sweden's Riksbanken, is founded.

Late 1600s: The flag is now a symbol for the country, not just the king.

1709

1709: Involved in the Great Northern War since 1700, Karl XII loses the Battle of Poltava against Peter I of Russia, which means the beginning of the end for Sweden as a great power.

1710–1713: The plague kills about one-third of the populations of Stockholm, Gothenburg and Malmö.

1719

1719–1772:
The Age of Liberty

1719: A new constitution that weakens the king's role and clearly outlines the role of the government and parliament makes the Swedish government the most democratic in the world.

1721: The Swedish empire falls as the Baltic provinces become Russian through the Treaty of Nystad.

Mid-1700s: Booming iron production and textile industry lead to labor immigration from Germany, Denmark, Holland, England and France as new skills are needed to run factories and machines.

1766

1766: Sweden introduces the world's first Freedom of the Press Act.

Olaus Petri, chancellor under Gustav Vasa for a short period and preacher in the cathedral, started using Swedish in his services.

Gustav II Adolf

Sweden expands around the Baltic Sea.

Karl XI on a SEK 500 bill today.

The impressive Wrangel Palace in Stockholm in the 1660s. Copperplate by Erik Dahlberg from Suecia Antiqua et Hodierna, *a collection of 353 engravings published in the 1720s.*

1544   1611   1658   1660

1527 onwards: Sweden breaks with the pope—the Reformation. The Catholic Church loses its secular power in Sweden, but Catholicism coexists with Protestantism for a long time.

1544: Hereditary monarchy is introduced.

1593: The Swedish church becomes officially Lutheran/ Protestant.

Mid-1500s: 1.3 million inhabitants in Sweden-Finland. Exports from Sweden: iron, copper.

1611–1721: Sweden a great power

1611: King Gustav II Adolf co-rules the country with Lord High Chancellor Axel Oxenstierna, who organizes the administration of Sweden and makes a name for himself in Europe.

1628: The warship Vasa sinks on her maiden voyage, just after leaving Stockholm harbor.

1645: Sweden's first weekly newspaper, *Ordinari Post Tijdender,* later *Post- och Inrikes Tidningar,* is published (the world's oldest still published newspaper, but now only on the web).

1617–1658: Sweden expands around the Baltic Sea. After the Peace of Roskilde in 1658, Sweden is at its largest. It took Sweden less than a century to go from poor, backward, unknown state to great European power.

Mid-1600s: 3 million inhabitants in the whole realm of Sweden.

1660: Karl XI becomes king at the age of 4; later military dictator, but also a man of peace, reconstruction and organization.

Gustav III founds Sweden's first opera on Gustav Adolf's Square in Stockholm. Inaugurated in 1782.

The sculptor Johan Tobias Sergel is ennobled in 1808. Self-portrait.

Scene from the film The Emigrants *by Jan Troell.*

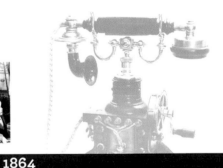

1786   1809   1842   1864

1772–1809: The Gustavian Age

Freedom of religion is expanded—Jews and Catholics are allowed to settle in Sweden and keep their religion, but with restrictions as to professions and where to live.

1786: The Swedish Academy is founded to work for the "purity, strength and nobility" of the Swedish language. The profession of writer is placed at the top of the social scale.

1789: Six months before the French Revolution, the first leveling of the estates— nobility, clergy, burghers and peasants—takes place, through which new advantages and perquisites are given to non-noble estates. Peasants begin their political and economic journey.

1809: Finland becomes independent from Sweden after invasion by Russia in 1808.

1809: Sweden becomes a constitutional monarchy, where power is shared between the king, the council and the parliament. Legislative power is shared by the king and the estates. The Parliamentary Ombudsman becomes Sweden's first ombudsman in the modern sense of the word.

1814: Norway is forced into a union with Sweden under Karl XIII. Lasts until 1905.

1842: Compulsory education (for 7 to 13-year-olds) is introduced.

Mid-1800s: Life expectancy in Sweden is 41 for men, 44 for women; average height for men 165 cm (5 ft 5 in, compared to 6 ft today).

1850–1930: 1.3 million Swedes emigrate, mainly to North America.

1862: The main national railway between Stockholm and Gothenburg is opened.

1864: Freedom to pursue any trade is introduced, preparing the ground for the Swedish market economy.

1876: Lars Magnus Ericsson opens a telegraph repair shop— and so his namesake communications company is born.

Early 1900s: Life expectancy in Stockholm is 39 years for men, 47 for women (53 and 54 in the countryside). More than 5 million inhabitants in Sweden, despite the large emigration.

1906: Ericsson's main telephone plant has almost 1,500 employees.

Elin Wägner next to 350,000 signatures for women's suffrage.

Prime Minister Hansson leads a demonstration during World War II.

Dag Hammarskjöld

Olof Palme

1918 **1932** **1939** **1944** **1946** **1979** **1986** **1990** **1995**

1918–1921: First all men, then all women get the right to vote.

1932: Prime Minister Per Albin Hansson starts 40 years of Social Democratic government. The concept of *folkhemmet* (literally: the people's home) leads the way for the Swedish welfare state and the Swedish Model.

1939–1945: Sweden remains neutral during World War II, but the Swedish press is censored and Germans and German weapons are permitted to be transported through Sweden to Nazi-occupied Norway. Foodstuffs are rationed and surrogate products appear.

1944: Swedish diplomat Raoul Wallenberg saves a large number of Jews from the Nazis in Budapest, Hungary. And at the end of the war, Folke Bernadotte, member of the royal family, achieves the release of 21,700 people from German concentration camps through negotiations.

1946: Sweden joins the United Nations. Swedish Dag Hammarskjöld is Secretary-General of the UN 1953–1961. After World War II Sweden is transformed into one of Europe's leading industrial nations.

1979: Sweden is the first nation to prohibit all corporal punishment of children.

1980: Female succession to the throne comes into effect.

1986: Social Democratic Prime Minister Olof Palme is assassinated in central Stockholm.

Early 1990s: A bursting real estate bubble combined with an international recession leads to a financial crisis.

1995: Sweden joins the European Union.

1999: New legislation criminalizes those who purchase sex.

Flags of Sweden and the European Union.

Gender-neutral weddings in 2009.

Crown Princess Victoria gets engaged to long-time boyfriend Daniel Westling in 2009.

2000 **2001** **2008** **2009** **2020**

2000: The Öresund Bridge between Sweden and Denmark opens.

2001 (and 2009): Sweden chairs the EU.

2003: Foreign Minister Anna Lindh is assassinated in central Stockholm.

2003: Swedes vote no to the euro in a referendum.

2008: The Swedish parliament passes the FRA law, which gives the Swedish National Defence Radio Establishment the right to wiretap all telephone and internet traffic that crosses Sweden's borders, as an anti-terrorism measure.

2008: New labor migration policies make it easier to move to Sweden for work for non-EU/EEA and non-Nordic citizens.

2009: Gender-neutral marriages are approved, both religious and non-religious.

2009: Eighty-nine percent of Swedes aged 16 to 74 have access to internet at home, and 86 percent use internet at least once a week.

2020: Ninety percent of all households and companies in Sweden should be able to communicate with a speed of at least 100MB/second, according to the government's broadband policy.

Megalithic monument or Iron Age ship setting? Researchers debate the origin of Ale's Stones in the south of Sweden.

The Öresund Bridge has moved Sweden even closer to Europe.

Rikard Lagerberg is a writer and editor who has spent most of his adult life in the US and on Ireland. Returning to Sweden he discovered a new curiosity for his native country. Editor and writer Emma Randecker spent most of her life in Sweden, apart from a couple of longer excursions to France and the UK. It was, in particular, a longing for the changing Swedish seasons that made her go back home after a few years. Both Rikard and Emma work at the Swedish Institute.

© 2010, Rikard Lagerberg, Emma Randecker and the Swedish Institute

The authors alone are responsible for the opinions expressed in this publication.

Graphic design: Patric Leo
Paper: Algro Design Duo 360 g (cover), ProfiMatt 150 g (inside)
Printed in Sweden: Edita Västra Aros AB, Västerås, 2010
ISBN: 978-91-520-0991-8

SWEDISH INSTITUTE
Sharing Sweden with the world

The Swedish Institute (SI) is a public agency that promotes interest and confidence in Sweden around the world. SI seeks to establish cooperation and lasting relations with other countries through strategic communication and exchange in the fields of culture, education, science and business.

SI works closely with Swedish embassies and consulates around the world.

Sweden.se, Sweden's official website, is operated and developed by SI. The site invites visitors to read about and experience contemporary Sweden in many different languages.

Sweden Bookshop has a wide range of books about Sweden and Swedish fiction in around 50 languages. The bookshop can be found at Slottsbacken 10 in central Stockholm and at www.swedenbookshop.com.

The Swedish Institute
Box 7434   +46-8-453 78 00
SE-103 91 Stockholm   si@si.se
Sweden   www.si.se

Do you have any views on this SI publication? Feel free to contact us at books@si.se.